The Soul
of an Immigrant

CONSTANTINE M. PANUNZIO

Arno Press and The New York Times

NEW YORK 1969

THE SOUL OF AN IMMIGRANT

THE MACMILLAN COMPANY
NEW YORK · BOSTON · CHICAGO
DALLAS · ATLANTA · SAN FRANCISCO

MACMILLAN & CO., Limited
LONDON · BOMBAY · CALCUTTA
MELBOURNE

THE MACMILLAN CO. OF CANADA, Ltd.
TORONTO

THE
SOUL OF AN IMMIGRANT

BY

CONSTANTINE M. PANUNZIO
Author of "The Deportation Cases of 1919-1920"

New York
THE MACMILLAN COMPANY
1928

COPYRIGHT, 1921,
BY THE MACMILLAN COMPANY.

Set up and printed. Published September, 1921.

Reissued November, 1924

Press of
J. J. Little & Ives Company
New York, U. S. A.

TO ALL

ACKNOWLEDGMENTS

English poetry has materially helped the author of this book to understand the genius of the Anglo-Saxon mind and character and of the soul of America. It is therefore fitting that he should, and he does hereby, make acknowledgment of his indebtedness to the poets quoted in this book and to the publishers for having accorded him the right to use copyrighted material. In particular to The Macmillan Company for the citations from the poetical works of Arnold, Byron, Cowper, Vachel Lindsay, Tagore, Tennyson, and Wordsworth; to Messrs. Charles Scribner's Sons and to Doctor Henry Van Dyke for the quotations from "The Poems of Henry Van Dyke"; to William Herbert Carruth for the stanza from "Each in His Own Tongue"; to the *Ladies' Home Journal* and to C. Austin Miles for the music to Doctor Van Dyke's "America for Me," and to George H. Doran Co., and Christopher Morley for "The Madonna of the Curb"; to Harcourt, Brace & Co. and Thomas Daly for "Da Little Boy"; to B. W. Huebsch and Percy MacKaye for the lines from "The Immigrants"; to the John Lane Company and W. J. Dawson for the selection from

"America"; to Little, Brown & Co. and Denis A. McCarthy for "The Land Where Hate Should Die"; to Messrs. Lothrop, Lee & Shephard and Richard Burton for the quotation from "Lyrics of Brotherhood"; to Houghton Mifflin & Co., for the lines from Phœbe Cary; to the *Nation*, to Rainer Maria Rilke, and to Ludwig Lewisohn (translator) for "Concerning Great Cities"; to the Frederick A. Stokes Company and Alfred Noyes for the quotation from "The Avenue of the Allies"; to the G. Schirmer Music Stores, Los Angeles, for the citation from Donizetti's "Italia Beloved," and to Messrs. A. P. Watt & Sons and Rudyard Kipling for the two stanzas from "The Stranger."

FOREWORD

DURING the winter of 1905-1906 I was attending a preparatory school in the State of Maine. One cold night a schoolmate, now professor in a Southern university, came into my room and, throwing himself upon my bed, somewhat abruptly asked me to tell him how I happened to come to the United States. I have no way of knowing what put the idea into his mind; it may have been, and perhaps it was, mere boyish curiosity. It was past midnight when he left the room; and then only in answer to the uncanny cry of the watchman: "All lights out." My friend returned to my room repeatedly after that, and, though at times annoying me, managed, little by little, to wring out of me the "round unvarnish'd tale."

Since that night I have had to tell the story hundreds of times to audiences varying from one person to hundreds of men and women, and from Bath, Maine, to Salt Lake City, Utah. Naturally the tale has grown somewhat longer in the meantime and has acquired many more twists. Everywhere it has evoked interest and, what is far more important, has awakened sympathy toward the "foreigner." After a time, however, it became both embarrassing and tedious for me to repeat the story, and I sought a way of avoiding my doing so. America's entrance into the War at last brought me relief for thereby I was able to break all engagements.

With the close of the War, however, and with the unprecedented way in which the American public has turned its attention to the all-important question of the assimilation of the immigrant, it became increasingly clear to me that I owed it to my adopted country to give the story to the public. Scores of persons had told me that I owed this as a matter of duty; but I had turned a deaf ear primarily because it is so personal and it goes so deep into the very recesses of my being. A teacher-friend at last made me realize that if the story were to do any good it need to go out at this time; so I have given it to the public.

The story is a simple one; it is that of a sailor lad who nineteen years ago to-day left his native country and through a series of strange incidents came to the United States and through another series of strange circumstances came definitely and consciously to adopt America as his country. What happened during this period; how he found his way into the immigrant community, how he secured his first "job," how he was ensnared into peonage, how he was robbed and then dragged into a prison, how he was led into unlawful acts, how he freed himself from the grip of unscrupulous peoples, how he struggled to secure an education, to get naturalized and to fit into American life; these and many other experiences, typical of thousands of immigrants in this country, are told frankly and boldly.

If the narrative has any particular value it grows out of the fact that it recounts the struggles of an *average immigrant*. It is not the life story of a Jacob Riis, an Andrew Carnegie or an Edward Bok that is told here, but that of an immigrant lad who has been neither too successful nor too unsuccessful. The stories of great and successful immigrants have led some Americans to say: "See what great people immigrants are! We need more of them"; while others, equally as superficially, have said: "If these immigrants have been able to make such a mark for themselves in our world, *all* immigrants could do the same if they wanted to." Both of these statements are beautiful, but what they imply is not true to fact. This story suggests—and I hope in a constructive manner—what helps or hinders *the many* in or from becoming useful American citizens.

Again, this tale depicts *the inner, the soul struggles* of the immigrant more than his outward success or failure. It tells of the agonies and the Calvaries, of the bitter sorrows and the high joys of an immigrant soul; it traces the liberation of a mind from the conceptions it brought from the Old

World and pictures its development into the American consciousness. Not outward poverty, degradation, misery; but inner conflict, soul-struggles are here primarily depicted.

Moreover, this is the story of an *Italian boy*. Several immigrant autobiographies have been written in the last twenty-five years, but I know of only two that are by men of Italian birth. We Italians by birth are so proud of our native land that, even though we become fully Americans at heart we may hesitate to publish the fact broadcast. I too have had to face this conflict, but my gratitude to America has led me frankly to indicate the benefits I have derived from residence in the United States.

Then also, this is the autobiography of a *South-Italian*. Regarding the South-Italian many unpleasant things are being hinted at, if not openly expressed, in these days. This story shows that even a southern Italian can make something of himself under the inspiring influence of America, when he has the proper opportunity and is thrown in the right environment.

These are the reasons why I have written this book. It has been far from easy for me to do so. It goes so deeply into the very recesses of my consciousness, it recounts so many unpleasant and humiliating experiences, that, frankly, I should have preferred not to have written it at all, or to have permitted it to appear in the cold blackness of

print. But I have done both as an offering to my
adopted country. I have told the story frankly,
fully; sometimes I think *too* frankly, *too* fully. If ·
that be considered a fault, let it be laid against my
desire to be of greatest possible service to my country, America, regardless of the way it may affect
me personally.

Some of the chapters I have left pretty much in
the form in which my original notes were, notes
made at the time of the events narrated; I have
done this in order that I might give a truer picture of the struggle in point and not mar the original
impression by throwing upon it the light of later
knowledge or development. I am aware that the
language is not always in the form in which it should
be. In this as in other respects I could be my own
most scathing critic. I ask the indulgence of the
reader, however. For after all my only desire is
that this little book may help Americans to understand, a little more fully perhaps, what fire the immigrant passes through as he lifts his face toward
the real America.

I owe a debt of gratitude to a number of persons
who from time to time have counselled me in regard
to this book. I here express my thanks to them all;
particularly to Professor Robert E. Park of the
University of Chicago and to Miss Mabel A. Brown
of Remsen, N. Y., who examined this book in its preliminary form and made valuable suggestions. I

wish to mention especially Bishop and Mrs. Fred B.
Fisher, of Calcutta, India, who not only have been of
greatest help in connection with this work, but who
also through the undying loyalty of years have been
of greatest inspiration to me; also Mr. Theodore A.
Hildreth of White Plains, New York and Miss Lenore
M. Ryan of Berkeley, California, who in a like manner have been a profound spiritual influence.

C. M. PANUNZIO.

White Plains, N. Y.
May 3, 1921.

CONTENTS

A NATIVE OF ANCIENT APULIA

Like tides on a crescent sea beach,
    When the moon is new and thin,
Into our hearts high yearnings,
    Come welling and surging in—
Come from the mystic ocean
    Whose rim no foot has trod—
Some of us call it Longing,
    And others call it God.
                    William Herbert Carruth.

THE SOUL OF AN IMMIGRANT

CHAPTER I

A NATIVE OF ANCIENT APULIA

I N that division of southern Italy known to the
ancients as "Apulia," about twenty miles north
of Brindisi, the Brindisium of Roman days, a
quaint old city slumbers peacefully beside the placid
waters of the blue Adriatic. It bears the name of
"Molfetta." To what age this little city goes back
no one can tell. It is evident, however, that it is
very old. In the heart of it the remains of what
was once a walled citadel are still to be seen. The
massive wall, some thirty feet high and three feet
thick, with its old gates and doors, still stands. The
queer, narrow, alley-like streets, with overhanging
arches here and there; the low, flat-roofed dwellings,
with their outside walls standing unceremoniously
right on the streets; the little public squares, which
are not squares at all,—all speak of the age of the
town. The Saracens at one time occupied this village, and have left their traces, both in the architectural form of the town and in the blood of the people.

Three high Byzantine towers were still standing at the time this story begins; two of them still rise, like silent sentinels of past ages, above what is the oldest Christian church in the town. The third once lifted its head as a clock tower above the Great Gate. The citadel, however, goes back farther than the Saracens, to the time when Roma was mistress of the world.

An interesting legend is recounted to this day by the inhabitants of Molfetta, which throws some light on the age of the ancient village. When Hannibal was ravaging this part of Italia Antica, so the story goes, the populace became greatly alarmed and fearing an attack, were driven into a state of panic. The Roman centurion in command of Molfetta, to calm their fears, called the people together one day in the public square to address them. There was in the little town a very large man, a veritable giant; with him the centurion had arranged to carry out a scheme to restore their courage. As the people assembled, the giant came with them. The centurion made his speech, in the course of which he said:

"Citizens of Molfetta, have no fear of the enemy; we are strong enough to defeat him; in fact there is one man in this very assembly who alone can put the enemy to flight."

Just then he beckoned to the giant, who came forward. "This is the man," said the centurion, pointing to him.

The people, the legend continues, looked at each other in astonishment, wondering how this one man could defeat the army of the mighty Carthaginian. Obeying the orders of the officer, the giant, unarmed, strode out from amid the crowd and made his way to the outskirts of the village. The people looked on in amazement. Going out a mile or two from the village, the giant lay by the roadside awaiting the approach of the enemy. When he saw them coming, so the story narrates, he rolled himself in the dust of the roadway and began to utter the most unearthly howls and screams. When the commander of the invading army, marching at the head of the column, came up to him, he stopped his horse and asked what was the trouble. The giant promptly answered, with cries and still more cries, that because he was *the smallest man* in the town, the inhabitants had driven him out in order that he might not be in their way when the fighting should take place. Needless to say the mighty Carthaginian army was at once ordered to retreat and hastily made its way from the outskirts of Molfetta.

Around the ancient citadel about which this and many other interesting legends are woven, lies the modern Molfetta, known as "Molfetta nuova," in contrast to "Molfetta vecchia." This is comparatively a modern town, as modern towns go in southern Italy. The streets are wider, the houses are more pretentious, built in the Roman style with their "antria"—open courts—in the center. The principal street of the town, known as the "Corso," runs in a straight line north and south, parallel to the coast and just outside of the ancient wall. Along this street are all the principal shops, stores, offices, cafés and clubs; farther along its course are the few monuments and public buildings which adorn the town; monuments to Victor Emanuel, Mazzini, Garibaldi, Cavour; the Cathedral, the Municipal Theater, the public baths and the Villa Garibaldi, or public garden. To the east of the Corso and north of the old wall, lies the "porto" or harbor, almost asleep in its inactivity, with perhaps a round hundred masts of coasting schooners and fishing skiffs raising their heads above the tranquil waters. In the outskirts of the city are the only industrial establishments, supported by the population of some 40,000 souls; a soap shop, two macaroni factories, and an electric plant. Farther out is to be found the cemetery, in some ways the most beautiful place in town, with its scores of little private chapels, real gems of architecture, and the never-dying pale glow made by myriads of little oil lamps, keeping their eternal vigil over the souls of the dead.

The country surrounding Molfetta is one of varied beauty. The main highways, some of which can be traced back to ancient times, are well kept. Endless rows of tall, slender trees make the scene picturesque and beautiful. The whole countryside is a paradise of orchards of orange and lemon trees, of fig, almond, olive, peach, pistaccio, walnut, and others, while grape vines are present everywhere.

The life of the people is very simple. The climate, which nine months of the year is very mild, gives them a leisurely attitude toward life. They live in comparative poverty, gaining their entire livelihood from the products of the soil. They are overburdened with taxes, which reach down to the least article they wear or consume. But even in their poverty they are happy, for their poverty is not placed in bold contrast with enormous riches on every side, as is the case in some countries. The town is seldom visited by tourists and the people live in a little world all to themselves, scarcely ever troubling their minds with the events of the outside world or even of other parts of Italy.

Their main diversions consist in the various social and religious festivals of the calendar year. First comes the Carnival, when the whole population indulges in a season of play and carousing, moral and immoral. This is followed by Passion Week, with its somber night processions, culminating in the gladsome celebration of Easter. On Corpus Christi day the whole city is one panorama of flowers and bright colors. Rich and poor alike hang out of their windows their best quilts and silk spreads, covering the walls of the streets with the bright hues. From far and near the best flowers of the season are brought in and thrown along the streets on which the procession passes. San Corrado, the patron saint of the city, has his day on the 8th of August. The streets are decorated and illumined profusely, and a large quantity of fireworks are lighted at night. On September 20th comes the national holiday commemorating the independence of Italy. Orations, illuminations and fireworks are the order of the day. Finally comes Christmas, the one festival season of all the year when the people are truly in a spirit of worship.

Aside from these feasts and celebrations, the townspeople have little of a social character. The town maintains a municipal theater which is open for two or three months in the winter. In the summer the band gives concerts in the Villa Garibaldi. There are few, if any, community dances or functions, and seldom do the people go out on picnics or social functions of a similar character.

It was in this city and in this environment that I first saw the light of day. The family of my father traces its history back to the twelfth century and to a French monk. It is said that this monk grew weary of the warm comforts and the leisure of monastic life, and abandoned the monastery for the cold realities of life. He married and established a family of his own in northern Italy. Later his descendants went down into the sunnier clime of southeastern Italy, where they have lived for centuries. Here they built for themselves an enviable record, rising to the ranks of petty nobility and giving to Italy many professional men.

I was born and lived in old Molfetta the greater part of my youth. I do not know the particular house in which I was born, but one thing is certain: there was great rejoicing in the home of my parents on the day of my birth. This was not due to the fact that a *child* was born, but rather that a *boy* had come into the world.

In the background of this extraordinary rejoicing was this story. From what grandmother told me over and over again even when I was a mere babe, it seems that my paternal grandfather had been a man of unusual character and personality. Don Costantino, as he was known, had been a physician by profession, and as was often the case in that day, he had also practiced law. It is said that in both capacities he had rendered great service, especially to the poor. What seems to have given him a special place in the hearts of the people of his native Molfetta and raised him to the realm of a household god, however, was his ardent patriotism. During the middle of the nineteenth century, Italy, and especially southern Italy, was in the iron grip of the Bourbons, the worst tyrants of the time. In the early revolutions of 1848-1849, when the foundations of a United Italy were being laid, grandfather seems to have been the moving spirit of a small group of patriots, who had banded themselves together in a secret organization, determined to arouse and lead the people of Molfetta and the surrounding villages to do their part in the cause of liberty. Spies, everywhere the worst enemies of progress, were as thick as vermin. They soon discovered this small band of patriots, and in a raid conducted under the dark cloak of night, they arrested Don Costantino and fourteen others and without trial hastened them to the notorious dungeon of Montefusco, near Naples, where many patriots had found death. Grandfather, being the leader, was singled out and forced to drink a cup of poison. When he realized that the end had come he is said to have uttered these as his last words: "My poor children and my country!" His co-conspirators who had been seized with him were brought in to view his stiffened body and were told that they too would suffer a like end, unless they would promise to give up their revolutionary tendencies and become "orderly and honorable citizens." Then they were released.

Grandfather's widow was left without resources to bring up a family of six children. In 1870, when Italy was at last free and had become a united and independent kingdom, grandmother received a pension, which on her death passed to my father, and when he died it reverted to me. Poor as I have been, I have never collected a centime of it. Thus the irony of history was repeated in grandfather's case: one day an "established" order wounds, outlaws or slays, on the morrow another equally "established" order extols to the sky, erects monuments, makes heroes and saints.

The connection between this story and the special rejoicing over the event of my birth lay in this:—at last the family had a boy who would perpetuate the name of its ancestor-hero. Two boys and four girls had been born previous to my coming, but although all the girls had lived, the boys had both died and the family was beginning to fear that the name of their hero would not be perpetuated. It was, then, purely a matter of ancestor worship. Accordingly, I was named and on the fifth day of my earthly journey I was christened "Costantino." In this manner the task of carrying on grandfather's name and reputation was placed upon my slender shoulders and my yet unborn consciousness.

Grandmother was the controlling factor of my early life; she took charge of my bringing up even while I was being nursed. She immediately set herself the task of making a second grandfather out of me. Evidently she was not to be satisfied with my bearing his name only; I was to be his exact duplicate! To that end she began to tell me the story of her martyred husband's life and death. Even before I could possibly have understood what she was saying, she wove that story into my infant consciousness so strongly that the first time I became conscious of my existence it seemed that I was not I, but grandfather re-born in me. My earliest memories are those of sitting in grandmother's lap in the gentle hour of twilight, and hearing each night the bedtime story of my hero grandfather. She would then put me to bed and, gently kissing me goodnight, would almost invariably say: "Tu devi divenire un grand'uomo, come il tuo nonno"—"You must become a great man, like your grandfather."

As I grew older dear grandmother went still further; she worked out a plan for my life to the last detail. "First a priest, then a teacher, and at last a patriotic statesman," she would say. Then she proceeded to carry out the plan. She even went to the extent of choosing a baby girl, a distant relative, as the one who should some day become my wife. Thus while I was barely a midget, I was betrothed.

In her plans, however, my grandmother did not take into consideration the great laws of heredity, as I presume many grandmothers do not. She of course was not to blame; in her day not much was known on this subject, and even in our times we are just beginning to unfathom the great mystery. But we shall presently see that some other being than my paternal grandfather presided at my conception and, at least in my youth, directed the course of my life. And perhaps it was due to the conflict be-

tween the powers of heredity on the one hand, and
the plan of life as worked out by my grandmother
and all my relatives, on the other, that on a not far-
distant day I was to find myself in the country
beyond the setting sun, there to become an American.

But that is getting a bit ahead of the story. We
must return to my family and to the general background of what follows. My father was the oldest
of the six children left for grandmother to bring
up. Although without means, in keeping with the
custom of the time regarding the education of the
oldest son, she managed to send my father to the
University,—in itself an extraordinary feat for a
woman in those days, and even to-day, in Italy.
Father followed the usual classical course of the
time, and upon his graduation, became instructor
in jurisprudence, and later in life took up the practice of law in his native city, Molfetta. At one time
in his life, I am not certain just when, he established
and conducted a private boys' school. In this he
seems to have done his best work, for to this day
there are not a few men in Molfetta and in other
parts of Italy, and occasionally I have run across
one in America, who revere his memory as that of
a beloved teacher. Father took an active interest
in public life; occasionally he wrote articles on
patriotic and civic subjects. He had a fair amount
of ability as a public speaker, which he devoted to
the service of his country, especially against all

forms of corrupt politics, of which he was a mighty foe. In Molfetta, Don Colì (an abbreviation of Don Nicolino) as he was known, was respected and honored chiefly for his sturdiness, his courage, his integrity and his sense of honor.

In his home father was primarily law and secondarily love. Although I lived with grandmother I came under the influence of both. In fact, on account of my being the eldest son and the one who was to perpetuate grandfather's good name, father took special pains with me. In the exercise of his function as law giver, father made use of two methods; that of being a teacher and that of applying the rod. He was first and last the "pater familias," whose word could seldom be questioned, and never disputed. He taught us many Latin and Italian proverbs, dealing primarily with outward conduct and good manners. Most of these were of a negative, or *don't-you-do-this-or-that* type. He was anxious that we should bear ourselves honorably in life, mainly emphasizing obedience and good behavior as well as respect toward authority and to the aged.

I remember him more vividly as an applier of the rod, however, simply because of the *impressions* he made upon me in that way. That he sometimes resorted to severe forms of punishment I have no doubt, though I suppose, in keeping with the usual custom, I should laud the punishments which I re-

ceived in my youth. He would often tie me to a
bed post and keep me there for hours. Once, for
having stayed away from school a day, he locked
me in a room, with big nails driven in the door, to
prevent mother from coming to my rescue. He kept
me there on bread and water for a whole week. Of
course I had more than just bread and water, for
dear mother managed to slip me something every
day by means of a long pole from the balcony of
the adjoining room. As far as he was concerned,
however, it was bread and water I had that week
and *no more*. My brothers as well as I came to fear
him greatly and often we would take refuge in the
home of some relative in order to escape his punishments.

And yet, strange as it may seem to one who did
not know him as we did, father was at times as tender
and gentle as a mother. Though he seldom played
with us, he loved us with a genuine and deep-seated
affection. I have very dear memories of the times
he used to take me for long walks in the country by
day and on the mole in the cool of the evening. At
such times I would catch glimpses of the sweetest
part of his nature. He used to love to go fishing,
and almost always would take me with him, revealing
then real tenderness and affection. He was as gentle
in the expression of his loving nature as he was
stern in the practice of his rod philosophy.

Mother was born of humbler parentage, and

therefore could not boast of a "Donna" before her name. But she was gentleness itself and the very embodiment of all that goes to make a truly noble woman. While yet quite young, she lost her father, who was captain and owner of a vessel, on the rocky and treacherous sea of Quarnero. This cast a veil of sadness over her whole life. But it was a sadness in which was interwoven a tenderness supremely sweet; it shone in her jet-black eyes and her delicately transparent face, which always beamed with a smile beneath her broad, noble forehead and her rich waving hair. She was stately in body, beautiful in soul, patient beyond compare, prudent and systematic in home management, ever busy with her large family, constantly sheltering us from the stormy nature of father, ever kind to servants, and gentle even to "Fanfù" our white pet dog, who had the unhappy faculty of making ever more work for her by tearing as many of our clothes as he could possibly get hold of. Mother's name was Angela and her face and character were those of an angel. She left an indelible impression upon the lives of us all.

There was one phase of my mother's life which gives me grief as I think of it. Because she was born of humble parentage, she was looked upon somewhat condescendingly by relatives on my father's side, most of whom lived not upon present merits, but in the glory of their heritage. Some

of them even went so far as to attempt to create
a similar attitude on the part of her children toward
her; but I am happy to say their efforts were in
vain, so deep was our love for mother. A similar
attitude was maintained by some relatives toward
an aunt of mine. Though she was a beautiful character, a woman of refinement and rare accomplish-
ments, because she was a native of Fiume and
therefore not an Italian, she was looked upon as a
despised "foreigner" by those members of our
paternal family who lived in the glory of the has-
been.

There were eight children in my father's home,
four sisters, all older than myself, and three brothers, all younger. We had a happy life together,
having pretty much the same kind of experiences
and the same kind of play-life as children do all
over the world. We were not privileged to have
many toys other than those of our own making.
My oldest sister had a complete set of delicate doll
house furnishings, but aside from this, I do not
recall that any of us had very much to play with.
We boys spent so much time in the out-of-doors
that the thought of toys never entered our minds.
Naturally, we sometimes had our quarrels, and I
seemed to have been the thorn in the flesh, especially
in the lives of my sisters. And yet we loved each other
profoundly. To one of my sisters, Agata, I took
a special fancy. Perhaps it was because she was

so different from the rest of us. She had hair which
was almost red, which would have puzzled the
eugenist to explain, for certainly there was none of
that particular tint or anything near to it in our
whole family. Agata was also different because of
her almost Irish sense of humor. She would make
us almost split our sides with laughter. She was
a very independent human being, insisting among
other things on choosing her own lovers without
reference to the wishes of the family. I remember
how enraged I became with one of her lovers for
capturing her exuberant and lovely affection.
Though I was a mere midget, I set out to punish
him, and meeting him by the Great Gate one evening,
I started to kick and to bite him.

While we all received instruction of various kinds,
dealing mainly with good manners and proper conduct, our religious education was very limited,
almost a negligible factor in our lives. Religion
was considered primarily a woman's function, unnecessary to men, and a matter about which they
continually joked. Even for the women of our
household, religion consisted simply in going to confession perhaps once a month and in going to mass
every Sunday. We children continuously heard our
male relatives speak disparagingly of religion, if
religion it could be called. They would speak of the
corruption of the Church. The men also complained
of the exorbitant expenditure of money in connec-

tion with the numerous feasts. Father might have
been called a "modernist." He had no particular
interest in the religious system of his town and
times, and although mother and grandmother were
very devout, I remember attending Sunday School
only once in all my boyhood days. Grandmother
would take me to mass and would talk to me about
becoming a priest, but it was most boresome to me.

We were taught the catechism in a perfunctory
way. The only religious reading I ever did as a
boy,—I was about ten years of age,—was once
when I was left alone in the house. I ransacked the
place, as boys will, and finally ran across a book
of "Bible stories." How such a book ever got into
our home I cannot say. I squatted myself down
on the floor and devoured some of the chapters.
All the while I was conscious of my wickedness in
reading such stories, but it did not occur to me that
my grandmother was sinful for having such a book
in her house. Even so, to me that reading was
most sweet. One of the stories was that of the
Resurrection of Jesus. It made a deep impression
upon my mind. It puzzled me; I could not figure
out how Jesus could walk again on earth after he
was dead. But I never let it be known that I had
read the story. I was afraid I would be punished
for reading the "Bad Book."

The relations between the various households of
our whole family were in the main most cordial. Ours

was a social existence as truly spontaneous and
beautiful as it was natural. All the long line of
relatives, uncles, aunts and cousins of every degree
lived in Molfetta. This gave us an opportunity for
much social intercourse. We had a custom of frequently getting together in the evenings for social
good times. The word would be given out that on
such an evening we were to meet in this or that home.
We generally began to assemble soon after supper,
and remained the entire evening, sometimes until
quite late. The women would immediately form
themselves into groups to discuss topics of interest
to them, while the men, who generally came later,
would gather about a table and play games. We
children would squat ourselves on the tiled floor
for frolic and games of our own. Occasionally we
would sing folk songs and patriotic airs. If the
accommodations afforded were sufficient, the adults
would dance. The children were seldom permitted
to join them except in the quadrille. It was never
necessary to import music for such occasions, for
our family, like every household in the length and
breadth of Italy, could boast of plenty of mu-
sicians. One played the guitar, another the mandolin, a third the flute, a fourth the cornet or
trombone. Pianos were rare in our homes; first,
because they were far too expensive, and then because they were not as "social" as the ready-to-
carry instruments. On some occasions the women-

folk would put aside their dignity and burst into
spontaneous frolicsome dances of their own to the
quaint music of the tambourine. At these times, we
had our greatest merriment. What a mirth-pro-
voking sight it was; we children would stand on
the "side lines" with sides almost splitting with
laughter, and I cannot refrain from bursting into
the same kind of laughter as I write these lines.

Usually "eats" and drinks were served by the
entertaining household; almonds, walnuts, raisins
and stuffed dates or figs, with home-made cakes and
candy. The best of the year's wine and "rosolio"—
a delicate liquor—were served. The children were
seldom allowed to touch the liquors, and then in a
much-diluted form. Frequently the beverages were
served after the children, tired with play, had been
put to sleep, a round dozen in each bed. Then the
adults would go on with "more interesting" subjects, which they would not discuss in the presence
of the children. More than once have I and some
equally daring cousin boldly crept out of bed to
take a peep or to listen through the keyhole and see
what was going on.

The party over, the children would be shaken
partly awake, and in the midst of much weeping
and wailing and gnashing of teeth, each family
would gather its brood and make its way through
the darkened streets toward their own homes. I for
one never troubled myself about the beautiful stars

of the Italian sky on such occasions, for I was generally in the land of I-am-still-asleep. Hanging to grandmother's arm and walking as in a trance, I would reach home as much in the land of Nod as though I had not been aroused at all.

These festive occasions generally took place during the more unpleasant months of fall and winter. For in the warmer months of spring and summer and early autumn, we, like everybody else, spent much of our time out-of-doors. For about six months of the year we went daily to the sea-baths; the invigorating salt baths making it unnecessary for us to have indoor bathrooms. For nearly nine months of the year the local band gave concerts in the Villa Garibaldi or on the Corso, and the people would throng to hear them. We would spend entire evenings taking a "passegiata," or leisurely stroll, up and down the Corso or by the quiet waters of the harbor. Invariably we would sit in groups around the marble-topped tables of the cafés to eat a "gelato" (ice cream), or to sip a delicious "orzata" —an almond drink. Occasionally a group would go for a launch ride on the peaceful waters; for sheer beauty and enjoyment these rides could scarcely be surpassed. Especially on a moonlight night, as was often the case, the balmy air, the gentle breezes, the melodious strains of the songs of southern Italy, and the sweet music of the mandolin or guitar wafted over the waters, made these truly enjoyable and memorable occasions.

In the summer we used to go to the country, especially at vintage time. I had an aunt who owned a large farm, and I was always invited there at grape-gathering time. It was the happiest season of all the year. I found my stomach limitless in its capacity for expansion. But best of all was watching the whole process of wine-making; the men and women, with bent backs, cutting the clusters from the vines with their tiny sickles; the enormous cane or wicker baskets which the women and girls carried on their heads; the big wooden vats, with men naked up to their loins madly tramping the grapes to extract the juices; the quaint skins in which the new wine was poured; the odd-shaped "water wagons" to haul the "juice" to the town. Most of all I loved to listen to the plaintive songs which the "contadini" would sing. All this made vintage time the most pleasurable season of all the year.

We had a wealthy distant relative who, though she managed to keep quite distant from all of us, occasionally invited me, the namesake of our family hero, to visit her at her villa in the country. The villa was one of artistic beauty, with its walls pure white, red-tiled roof and deep-green trimmings. A picturesque stone wall covered with creeping vines completely surrounded it. Long winding paths,

with rich pergolas overhanging them, led from the
road to the entrance. On either side and throughout the grounds a veritable paradise of flowers;
roses and tube-roses, carnations and lilies of every
variety, morning-glories and pansies wafted their
perfume through the balmy air. Stately trees arose
as sentinels about the villa, while here and there
throughout the grounds fountains gushed forth their
limpid waters and marble seats invited one to a life
of leisure. The villa was furnished most luxuriously
with costly rugs and vases and rare furniture from
many lands.

Not far from the villa and in bold contrast to it,
stood the crude huts of the "contadini." These
used to interest me greatly. They were cone-shaped
little dwellings made of rough stone or a mud mixture not unlike adobe. Each had a small opening
which served as a doorway, while the roof had a
small round hole which served as both window and
chimney. The floor was made of plain Mother
Earth; stones were the only chairs, straw the only
bed. In these huts lived the "contadini" who worked
on my relative's farm and made possible the up-keep
of the large holdings which she possessed.

Of all the seasons of the year, Christmas time was
perhaps the most beautiful for the people as a whole.
It was a season when a truly religious spirit pervaded every home. The weather was generally clear
and calm, the sun at mid-day bright and beautiful,

the skies of the night fathomless, the stars innumerable and bright as gems.

There was but little outward display at Christmas time. Save for the noise we boys made with the firing of fire-crackers and of rude little cannons of our own making, all was tranquil and peaceful. In the perfect stillness of the night the humble troubadours would wend their way from street to street, from alley to alley, singing their melodious carols to the quaint music of the bagpipe and the flute. For a few centimes they would stop beneath a window to chant their ancient songs, while the people lying in their beds would listen to the melody as to a chorus of unseen angels.

Christmas also was a time of real feasting. We had no Christmas trees or exchanging of gifts in Molfetta; in fact, we never knew of such a custom. True, we children hung up our stockings, but that was on St. Nicholas Day, the 5th of January, and instead of bothering with stockings, we preferred to hang up our adults' long-legged boots, which would hold much more. But so far as good things to eat were concerned, Christmas Day was the day of all the year. Every family, however poor, had a real feast. The very best of all the year's yield, kept for this occasion, would be brought forth. There were fruits of every kind; clusters of luscious grapes, quinces, pears, apples and pomegranates, long strings of figs, boxes of dates, and honey-dew melons

sweeter than honey; all would be disenthroned from
their lofty pantry dominions from which for months
they had been tempting the yearning eyes of children, and placed before all to have and to hold until
they could no more. Then there were big platters
of home-made candies and cakes, fritters and cookies
of every variety and shape, vegetables and meats
of every conceivable sort—my mouth waters even
now to think of the Christmas table of my childhood.

The Christmas dinner in our home was a memorable occasion not alone because of the good things
to eat, but also because of a special custom we had
of showing our gratitude to our parents. For days
before Christmas we would hunt high and low for
letter paper with the best decorations and mottoes.
Then we children would vie with one another in com-
posing the best letter or little poem to express our
love for mother and father. Before the Christmas
dinner, we would hide these in some place on the
table, perhaps folded in a napkin, under the plate
of father or mother, and even under the tablecloth.
Our parents would first pretend not to see them, and
would feign surprise when they were found, and the
best part of the Christmas dinner was to hear father
and mother read the letters we had written, and
then pronounce which one was the best.

On Christmas Eve the streets of Molfetta would
be lighted by myriads of dimly-burning lamps.
From every window of every house, however poor its

inhabitants might be, a small oil lamp would send forth its humble rays, until the whole town would be enveloped in a yellow haze of somber and subdued lights flickering their welcome to the Christ Child.

On Christmas Eve too, was held the Midnight Mass. I remember of attending only once, but the memory of it is as vivid as if I had attended on this very night. Within, the Cathedral was all a mass of dazzling light; candles flickered everywhere, even at the top of the pillars and on the uppermost cornices of the dome. Enormous candelabra with myriads of shining crystals cast their silver sheen upon the scene below. A purple velvet curtain hung from the top of the massive columns to the floor at the foot of the Great Altar, as if conscious of the stately dignity of its rich folds and golden fringes. Worshiping folk, young and old, rich and poor, thronged the church to its very doors. A spirit of quiet reverence pervaded all. As the midnight hour drew near, a deeper and more solemn stillness crept over the great throng. Just before the hour of twelve, a silver bell tinkled softly. The great audience became breathless and, as one man, bended its knees, remaining a few moments thus in silent adoration. My child eyes looked on in wonderment on this matchless scene. The curtain before the Great Altar slowly parted without a sound, as if opened by angel hands. Splendor was added to splendor. From the choir loft a viol began to weave

a gentle web of music. And now a voice was heard
softly chanting, then another and another, till of a
sudden the whole choir burst forth in jubilant song
as if a thousand thousand angel voices were swelling
their refrain. The trumpets of the great organ sent
forth sharp, joyous peals. It seemed as if Heaven
itself had come to earth to greet the New Born
Child. The audience then arose, joining in an
antiphonal song, after which the mass was said, and
the throng silently wound their way homeward beneath the brilliant sky of the midnight hour.

Impressive as was this event, there was something
which took place in the intimate circle of our home
which left a far more lasting impression. It was
the Presepio—the Manger. For days before Christmas Eve we boys would gather soil and sod, twigs
and branches, and bringing them to the house, with
boxes we would build a miniature Bethlehem. We
would make little houses and winding roads, and
plant little twig-trees until it looked like a natural
hillside. On Christmas Eve father would open a box,
which he kept sacredly locked all during the year,
and we would take out myriads—so it seemed to us—
of little terra-cotta figures, each representing a
character in the story of the Nativity. Under his
direction we would place each where it belonged; the
Magi just coming over the hill, with only the heads
of their camels showing; far in a corner of the room,
with a dim candle burning back of it, was the Star

of Bethlehem; over to the right were the Shepherds keeping their flocks by night; here were the people coming down the hill with their gifts; while near the floor was a little stable with Mary, Joseph and the Babe in the Manger.

Then father would gather all his children in a half-circle about the Presepio, mother in the center sitting in a small chair like the rest of us, and he would tell us the Story. A few candles cast a soft and gentle light upon the scene. With a long cane he would point to the various personages, and thus he would narrate to us the whole story of the birth of the Christ Child.

As I write these lines, it is Christmas Eve, and exactly twenty years since I last sat around the Presepio. Father and mother are gone to the land from whence there is no returning; the home of my childhood is no more, and I am in America, far, far from home. Sometimes, "like tides on a crescent sea beach" come longings for Italy and the scenes of my childhood.

THE CALL OF THE SEA

And I have loved thee, Ocean! and my joy
Of youthful sports was on thy breast to be
Borne, like thy bubbles, onward; from a boy
I wanton'd with thy breakers—they to me
Were a delight; and if the freshening sea
Made them a terror—'twas a pleasing fear,
For I was as it were a child of thee,
And trusted to thy billows far and near,
And laid my hand upon thy mane—as I do here.

George Gordon Byron.

CHAPTER II

I MUST have been very young when I was first sent to school. Molfetta maintained a public kindergarten, to which well-ordered families sent their children. The kindergarten was held in a very old building, once a monastery, which had been taken over by the government for school purposes. This was the only school building in the city and it housed all the school children from the kindergarten up through the elementary grades, as well as some of the "ginnasio" classes. I recall vividly the long dark halls and the endless lines of children seated on each side of long rows of tables, and playing with toys. I remember the tediousness of sitting day in and day out by one of those tables, and I can think of no particular contribution which kindergarten instruction made to my life. As I grew older I was sent to the elementary school, to which attendance is compulsory throughout Italy.

As I have already indicated, it was grandmother's plan, in which my father concurred, that I should prepare myself for a profession and thus follow in the footsteps of my grandfather. To that end,

I was to go through the elementary grades and on through the "ginnasio" and the "liceo" to the University. If a more scrutinizing eye had been watching the unfolding of my life, however, it would have observed that the winds were driving my bark, at least for the time being, in an entirely different direction. I do not wish to suggest that my father or my grandmother did not possess the average capacity for observation, but like many parents and relatives everywhere, instead of guiding the development of natural tendencies in child life, they tried to stifle them and to superimpose a cut and dried plan formulated long before my birth.

I must have shown a tendency for other than school and professional life from my earliest days. For even my kindergarten books were covered with crude drawings of ships. My grade-school books, still preserved by an aunt of mine, are, from cover to cover, one solid mass of ship pictures. At every opportunity I would run away to the harbor, to play by the water's edge or on the ships. When I was held in check, I used to go up on the roof of the house in which I lived with grandmother and cast my eyes longingly toward the water and the ships. In stormy weather it used to give me a feeling of special exaltation to watch the sailing skiffs driven before the wind. At night I would go up on the roof, and stretching myself flat on my back, I would look up into the infinite depths of that southern sky and count the stars or follow the

moon in her hastening course through the fleecy
clouds. My toys did not consist of blocks or sand
pile, but ships and everything that had to do with
the sea. My dreams at night were almost invariably of ships, of oceans and far countries. I
even dreamed sometimes that I could walk on the
waters and go to the countries beyond the horizon.
Cities of which I had heard or read became concrete realities in my mind's eye; I could have described some of them very minutely many years before my dream was realized and I actually saw
them. Every "soldo" or penny I could lay my hands
on was spent for little play-ships. I remember one
instance when fifty centimes worked an instanta-
neous miracle of healing. I was ill with some minor
ailment. My father came to see me and gave me
the money. That very afternoon I was perfectly
well again and might have been seen squatted on
the sidewalk fitting into place on one of my little
toy-ships some little riggings which the money had
bought.

The call of the sea was in my very soul, and in
proportion as it made itself felt, to that extent
all other interests were unconsciously being crowded
out of my boy life. School held absolutely no interest for me. I would rather any time spend my
days in or by the water than eat, to say nothing
of carrying a book under my arm, and I can actually recall spending whole days by the water side.
But the more that all-impelling power drove me,

the tighter was the circle of restriction drawn about me. Did I stay away from school to play by the beach, punishment was sure to follow at home, and to this was invariably added the punishment by my teachers. Of one I have a gruesome memory, because of the special forms of torture which he used. I remember that once he made me kneel on the desk platform for an hour or more with my hands under my knees. Another time he pinched my flesh between his fingers and twisting it, held it until I was exhausted and faint with pain. On still another occasion he locked me in a large room and left me there all night. All this because in each case I had been absent from school the day before.

But what of it? Was not an irresistible power driving my life, and could I be responsible for the direction in which it was leading me? It was the call, the call of the sea; the heaving, mighty sea, it was calling me.

At every opportunity I followed it. I clearly remember the first time I heard the call of a siren whistle. I must have been about ten years of age. One morning, long before rising time, I heard from the direction of the harbor an ugly noise. When the time came for me to start to school, my little feet led me in another direction. I went to the mole to see with my own eyes what kind of a monster was this which poured forth such frightful shrieks. Time passed and I forgot all about school; I loitered near the English coal freighter in the hope of hearing the siren blow again. There I remained until evening, my noonday luncheon standing me in good stead. I finally contrived to get on board the steamer and was about to make my way to some advantageous position from which I could examine with care the noisy instrument which had awakened me that morning, when I felt the grip of a mighty hand on the seat of my trousers, pulling me down with vengeance. I did not need to look to see who it was or what it was all about. I knew. It was my father. My absence from school had already been reported to him, and grandmother, too, had gone to him with her usual account of my non-appearance for my after-school lunch. My father "escorted" me home, but not with gentleness. And for weeks afterward I had livid recollections of the English coal freighter and its siren whistle.

In time I learned to sail a boat and I began to make frequent trips out upon the Adriatic. On more than one occasion I came near getting into serious trouble. One evening a school mate and I were sailing all by ourselves, when a stiff breeze caught our little boat and swept it along mercilessly. We did not know where we were going. Toward midnight we found ourselves almost upon the rocks near Trani, some fifteen kilometers from Molfetta. Just then a gust of wind flapped the sail over the mast and the boat all but capsized. How we managed to reach shore safely I cannot say.

As time went on I naturally became associated

with boys of like inclination, and soon found myself
the leader of a group, call it a "gang" if you will,
made up of sea-loving boys, whose one passion was
their belief in the sovereignty of the sea. Pattern-
ing our actions after the militaristic environment
in which we lived, we organized ourselves into a military unit. We had wooden guns and swords, and
wooden cannons properly mounted on wooden
wheels. We had our drills and maneuvers. One
day we were to meet to engage in mortal conflict
a gang of "land lubbers" whom we hated. We drew
up in military array in front of a little church in
Molfetta vecchia, ready for the onset. Our wood-
en swords covered with silver paper shone in the
sunlight. Our wooden rifles were lifted in air;
the national colors, made of tissue paper, waved
resplendently. The "fanfara"—bugle band—with
instruments made of contorted hands and wiggling
fingers, was playing. We were getting nervous and
eager for the battle, when to my utter amazement
I saw what looked like a gigantic figure coming
toward me. It was one of my uncles. He took me
by the ear and dragged me out from my position of
military importance at the head of my gang-bat-
talion. O, the humiliation of an officer being pulled
from his post in this manner! Who in all the an-
nals of warfare had ever heard of such a thing? Of
course I was punished, but neither the humiliation
which I suffered nor the punishment I received at
the hands of my uncle could compare with what

came to me a few days later, when some of the "enemy," enraged over my having been the cause of breaking up one of the most important battles of the season, saw to it that I got what they considered my just dues. Thus I suffered for my militaristic tendencies, for wanting to uphold the sovereignty of the sea on the one hand, and, on the other, for indirectly causing a period of peace to come over the neighborhood boys.

There were at least two occasions during the year when our sea-loving gang was liable to get into trouble. One of these was Carnival. Carnival was a time of special carousing in Molfetta and elsewhere. Almost every one went about in masquerade. Long, loose gowns, somewhat on the order of those worn by the Ku-Klux Klan, were the order of the day. Hoods with holes for the eyes were worn over the head. The women wore elaborate costumes, especially at the dances. But the most exciting part of Carnival, so far as we boys were concerned, came with the confetti. These were not the sham paper confetti such as are used at weddings in America, but real hard candy, sometimes filled with almonds or liquor. Although I generally had some difficulty in getting into costume because father did not approve of it, and grandmother was always afraid I would get hurt, I usually managed to get in with my gang. We would get hold of all the confetti we could and make the rounds of the homes of the girls who claimed our special attention. When they appeared on the balcony or at a window we would shower them with confetti. If a girl did not like us she would generally shut the window in our faces; whereupon, in keeping with custom, we would throw candy even more furiously than before, regardless of damage to the windowpanes.

At Carnival, we also tried to get in at some dance, at least as onlookers. My father was very strict about this and I scarcely ever attempted to go. Once I managed to get in at a public dance, but again a big man, my uncle, caught me by the ear, and I had to go.

The other occasion which usually brought the "gang" into some kind of difficulty was the feast of San Conrad, which comes in August. San Conrad is the Patron Saint of Molfetta, and is reported to have performed great miracles. It is a time of great feasting. The whole city is decorated. Along the Corso a continuous archway is built, draped with gay colors, and at night myriads of little oil lamps of different shades are lighted. During the morning there is a procession, and late at night there is a display of fireworks, lasing until near dawn.

One year while the fireworks were being displayed, our group of boys, roaming about from place to place, ran across a young cleric, a friend of ours. He suggested that an uncle of his had a large vineyard four or five kilometers out of town, and that if we wanted to, instead of going home after the fireworks, we could go out to the vineyard and have all the grapes we wanted. Without hesitating we acted upon his suggestion, and about one o'clock in the morning we started for the country. Toward dawn we reached a beautiful vineyard of white grapes. This, our young cleric informed us, was his uncle's place. We made short work of stripping a few vines of their luscious fruit, piling the grapes on our coats, which we had spread upon the ground. Then we sat in a circle and ate until we could eat no more. We played ourselves hungry again, and again we feasted on more grapes. It was now getting toward ten o'clock; and some one suggested that we had better return. We decided to do so, but it was agreed that we should generously provide ourselves with enough of the delicious fruit to last us at least until we should reach town. We filled our handkerchiefs and our pockets; we stored away grapes in caps and blouses. As we started on our way we heard shots fired into the air and saw the country police hot on our trail. Apparently they had been lying in wait for the right moment to pounce upon us. We called to our young cleric friend to come to the front and explain to the police that this was the vineyard of his uncle. But the cleric ran at double speed, one speed for our call and one to flee from the police. We all took to flight, throwing our grape-laden handkerchiefs as we went, emptying our caps and hats, our pockets and blouses, until the whole roadside was strewn with abandoned booty. Two other boys and I found ourselves together on a side road. We kept on running, stopping now and then to see if the police were following. Finally we caught up with a rack loaded with hay. We pleaded with the driver to let us hide in his load. We did so, but like the ostrich, we were simply waiting for our doom. The guards came up. Whether the driver gave us away we never knew, but we did find out that all three of us were in the hands of the "carabinieri" and were being taken to town. The policemen were deaf to our pleadings and promises of repentance—that repentance which is only sorrow for having been caught. They led us to police headquarters and our parents were notified. Toward evening my father came to pay my five-lire fine, and I was released. He took me home and then there was music; he surely took not five but a hundred-lire's worth out of me that night. More or less the same lot befell all the other boys.

As soon as we had sufficiently recovered from the flesh fines we had to pay and had again found our bearings, we called a special meeting in one of our secret holes back of the long mole. And then something else happened.

One evening, dark and dreary, we called our friend the cleric into compulsory association with us, and that night each of us took our five-lire's worth with compound interest out of his hide, and finished him up with a good ducking, in all his priestly robes, in the waters of the harbor. He promised never to do it again, and he never had the chance!

Another escapade cost me the sight of my right eye. As I have already indicated, it was a Christmas custom for boys to shoot off fire-crackers and other fireworks. One evening our gang secured a number of empty cartridges and some powder, and loading them, went from street to street firing them. In a "portone" it was my turn to touch the match to the fuse. Besides the powder the cartridge was loaded with stones to make all the noise possible. I lighted the match and in less time than it takes to tell it, the explosion took place and I was running at mad speed through the street totally blinded and in an agony of pain. Some one led me home. Father came home soon, having hea. he sad news. And he who was usually so stern was now melted with tenderness. I remember so well how he came to my bedside, bent over me and asked if I could see "papa's face." When I replied in the negative, he hugged and caressed me and burst into a torrent of tears. It seems as if I can still feel those tears dropping upon my face.

The retina of the right eye was broken and the sight permanently injured. Perhaps had the science of optometry been as far advanced in those days as now, my sight might have been saved.

Another event, added to all this, made every one

in the family, save mother and grandmother, conclude that I was a truly bad boy. This event was my running away from my first confession. On a given Sunday, Easter I think it was, I was to be confirmed. My dear grandmother spent weeks preparing for this occasion. The event interested me solely because of the new suit I was to wear, with my first long trousers, and because my aunt was making all kinds of special sweets. The thing itself, the coming confirmation, excited no concern in my mind. One afternoon during the week preceding the great day, I was taken by my aunt to our family priest, who looked after all our spiritual needs and ailments. I was to confess to him, and on the following Sunday my confirmation was to take place. It was early in the afternoon when we reached the church. We waited in the sacristy until the priest came out. After my aunt had chatted with him for a while, he took me by the hand and led me into a large dark room. In the center of it was a great throne-like chair, which I saw while the door was open. After the door was closed, he led me in the darkness to the chair, and seating himself in it, asked me to kneel at his feet. As I was in the act of kneeling, I suddenly became bewildered, and I was dazed. The door had not been completely shut and a streak of light came through the opening. Quicker than it takes to tell it, I was on my feet, had pushed the door open, rushed by my aunt, who looked on in open-mouthed wonder, and had gone out to play by the shore of my beloved sea. It was my first and only confession.

All these incidents, coming as they did within a period of about three years, led all my relatives, with the exception of mother and grandmother, to conclude that there was nothing good in the boy over whose birth they had so rejoiced. As I look back upon it now, I realize that it was only a natural rebellion against the fact that my relatives were attempting to crush out the strongest passion of my life. Father now took personal charge of me, and forgetting, or perhaps not understanding, the fundamental laws of life, he set out to *drive* from my mind the very thought of following the sea. He planned and carried out a definite punitive expedition into the territory of my growing youth. Like many parents, dear father mistook coercion for discipline and compulsion for guidance.

This was the way in which he attempted to turn my mind from the sea. In Molfetta, which at best is somewhat of a primitive society, castes are a part of the laboring world. There are certain types of work, especially all forms of manual labor, which are considered below the dignity of the best families, and which, if followed by any of them, constitute a disgrace. Now my father thought that by subjecting me to the humiliation of menial work, he could drive me back to school in a more sober state of mind. His abstract logic made him blind to Nature's all-compelling imperatives. He first put me to work in the foundry, then in the soap factory, in a blacksmith's shop, in a cobbler's place and in the electric plant. Strange as it seemed to all my relatives whose dignity was thus offended, I liked it. It meant new experiences, and it gave me opportunity to put into unrestricted use the creative powers of my youth. Then too, when I realized that I was earning money by the sweat of my toil, it gave me a sense of new life. Moreover, my earnings afforded me a chance to buy more things for my little ships. This experience gave me a new consciousness of freedom. Incidentally, it was while working in the soap factory, where we made Castile soap, which was shipped to America, that I had my first vague desire to visit some day that far-off country.

Realizing that this new tack was not bringing about the desired result, my father determined to force me to go back to school at any cost. For a long time he personally accompanied me to the school in order to make sure that I attended.

It was about this time that an opportunity came which, if utilized rightly, might have changed the whole course of my life, had my people but seen it. A certain Professor Rossi from northern Italy had interested a wealthy man, perhaps a native or former resident of Molfetta, to invest some money in the organization of a boys' band in our city. He sent down an expert teacher with full power to select forty boys, train them, supply them with instruments and uniforms, and lead them to success. I do not remember whether there was some form of an eliminating contest, nor how I came to be selected, but I was chosen to play one of the two first cornets. We were put through a period of intensive training, and as I recall it, in a remarkably short time were ready to make our first public appearance. For my part I was having a most delightful time and was behaving myself very well. But grandmother again stepped in to interfere. She may have thought that if I became too deeply interested in the band I would deviate from her well-planned scheme for my life. But whatever the reason, forgetting the cries of my childhood days, she insisted that playing the cornet was too hard for my lungs and that I must be taken out of the band, and she persuaded my father to do so. The band went on with its training, and soon made its appearance on the streets of the city. The whole town turned out to witness the event. The boys in their, to me, wonderful red uniforms, marched up and down the Corso amid the applause of the populace, and my eyes stuck out in envy, and my heart ached in utter misery. Subsequently, the band made a tour of the principal cities of Italy, winning several prizes and gaining national recognition. If there was any one thing which in my boyish heart I could never forgive grandmother for, it was her influencing my father to take me out of the band.

Notwithstanding all these boyhood struggles, I had managed by this time to pass all my grades and was ready to go on to the "ginnasio." Grandmother now directed that I should enter the Seminary where young boys were trained for the priesthood. In spite of all that had happened, the original plan whereby I was to become great was still ever-present in her mind: "First priest, then teacher, and then statesman." My father was decidedly disinclined to make a priest out of me, both because of his natural liberalism and because he knew too much of the corruption of certain institutions. Then too, he was becoming somewhat discouraged over the way my life was tending. Nevertheless, he consented, and I was placed in the Seminary.

To my boyish soul, with all its love for the open life, this was worse than everything else. It was like a dungeon to me, a tomb in which I found myself buried alive. The long corridors, the dark recitation halls, the cell-like dormitory rooms, were repulsive beyond comparison. Stone, cold stone everywhere, and not a breath of fresh air to breathe. To my nostrils, with the love of the exhilarating aroma of the sea, they smelled like catacombs. Around the whole enormous building was an iron fence some twelve feet high, with spearheads on the top. During recreation periods when we were allowed to go out on the narrow strip of ground around the institution, I would stand by the bars and look out longingly into the free world.

One evening I saw some of my boy friends playing near the Villa Garibaldi opposite, and I tried to get away. First I tried to scale the fence, but failing in this, I attempted to squeeze through the bars, only to find myself caught between them with my head out in the free world and my body unable to pass through. I became frightened and had to be pulled out by the "guardiano," or gateman.

More than the place itself I hated my teachers, especially my professor in mathematics! One night I came in with my lesson unprepared. He took me through one of those long dreary halls into a physiological and chemical laboratory, with all its horrible smells. Cunningly, he lighted a sulphur match. In the light of its ugly, purplish glow, he drew aside a curtain; before me stood a skeleton! It frightened me stiff, but it had no effect on the development of my mathematical bump. Later, one evening I came again with my lesson unprepared. In a fit of anger he split my head wide open with a ruler. With blood streaming down my face I ran to the gate, fought with the gateman and managed to escape. My father was furious, and for the first time he saw the way the winds of my life were blowing, and the absolute futility of forcing this sort of training upon me. He did not insist upon my returning, and that was the last of my school life in Italy.

The years covered by all these events were certainly tempestuous ones, and they came near proving fatal to my life. As I look back upon all that, consciously or unconsciously, I suffered in those tender years, I entertain no ill feelings. Rather, a feeling of great tenderness comes over me as I think of all the pain that I must have caused my parents and especially my dear grandmother, who had fastened all her hopes upon me for the perpetuation of what was to her a great family heritage. It was simply a matter of misconception of guidance, and for that they were not to blame. For they, like thousands upon thousands of people throughout the world, were blind to the inherited tendencies of life, and tried to force upon me a plan which was not in harmony with all those tendencies implanted within my soul long before my birth. They did not press their ear to my boy-soul; they did not hear what I heard, nor see what I saw. It was the call, the mighty call of the sea, the undying call for the larger life. And it was that call that in a not far-distant day was to lead me to America, there to find the opportunity for a true unfolding.

AMERICA

America, dear motherland of men,
Age after age lodestar of immigrants,
Hark to these peoples crying in the mist!
Here, where you loose your cities on the sea,
Leviathans of lightning—spire on spire,
Palace and hanging garden of the waves,
Whose spacious splendors house the lords of life—
Here, under all, cramped in their vitals, swarm
The seekers after life—the slaves of toil,
With hearts of yearning, O remember these—
And feed the awful hunger of their hearts!

Percy MacKaye.

CHAPTER III

I n the winter of 1897 I had reached the age of thirteen. My relatives, at last seeing the way the winds of my life were blowing, consented to let me go to sea. Securing a written permission from my parents, I applied for and received a sailor's pass book. Then I enrolled in the crew of a coasting schooner, the *Angelo*, as a "mozzo" (literally, "a stub") or sailor boy, and began to make ready for the great adventure which was ultimately to land me in America.

And now all that was beautiful and tender in the lives of my relatives was sweetly revealed. As after a period of sullen weather, Nature suddenly loosens her chilling grip and blossoms into radiant sunshine, so now all that had been curbing and repressive in their attitude became gladsome expression. The very persons who had vied one with another in declaring the sea-impassioned lad wayward, unruly and bad, now unloosed their deep-seated affection for me by doing all manner of things to make my approaching departure

[53]

a memorable event. One uncle bought a sea chest, and equipped it with all those little tools and trinkets so necessary to the life of a sailor; another made me a sailor bag, with funny eyelets and locks. One aunt contributed pillow slips and stockings; another gave me some fine woolen blankets; a third towels and handkerchiefs. Grandmother's heart was almost breaking. In the approaching departure of the boy of her love, she saw the fading forever of her dreams. Her gentle hands and her tender heart could not do enough; during that winter she wove her very soul into the stockings and underclothing which she knitted with her own hands, and into the thousand and one little things which she made to contribute to my comfort. Some of these things I have treasured through the years. She made me a small mattress and small pillows, soft as down, which fitted snugly into a large sailor bag, later to accompany me to America, where I was to lose them.

As spring drew near and with it the day of my departure, every one brought all kinds of eatables and tokens of love. On the day the ship left the harbor they all came to the mole to see me sail away toward the worlds of my dreams.

Toward sunset on the fifth of April, 1898, the *Angelo* raised anchor and spread her sails to a favorable breeze. The sea was smooth, the air was balmy, the sky clear as crystal. Molfetta was

wrapped in the splendor of the setting sun. The
Byzantine towers stood boldly out like mighty sentinels against the ruddy, western sky. With dusk
Molfetta began to fade until it died away in the
soft hues of the evening skies. I was leaving Molfetta destined to be hers no more!

The *Angelo* was bound for Fiume, a city which
of late has acquired international fame. On the
way we stopped at various ports either to avoid unfavorable weather or to take on provisions. The
first place we dropped anchor at was a natural cove
of unsurpassing beauty. A great rocky arm enclosed the waters so completely as to make the sea
without wholly invisible. Surrounding it like a
crown was a range of high mountains. On their
summit, the trees lifted their heads to the breeze,
while below the waters were wholly tranquil, save
for the gentle ripples made by the fishes jumping
here and there. Off in the distance was the only
sign of life: a fisherman's little hut on a small
beach. It was one of Nature's beauty spots, and
its virgin freshness and rugged grandeur left an
undying impression upon my boy-soul.

The awe-inspiring phenomenon of the mirages of
the Dalmatian Coast left also a never-effaced impression. No childish dream could possibly paint
a more fairy-like picture. The innumerable little
islands of that coast, with the few trees rising on
their crests, and the small fishing and merchant

ships were now and again lifted into the bosom of the heavens, making dream scenes realities. Our little ship often lay immovable upon its own reflection, the sails hanging lazily from the masts, more beautiful than any painted ship upon a painted ocean; while by day and by night Nature unfolded her matchless beauty about us in sunrise and sunset wonders and balmy weather. When, years afterward, I read "The Ancient Mariner," my mind instinctively went back to those matchless scenes of the Dalmatian Coast, to my first voyage, and to the first realization of the dreams of my childhood.

For a year and a half I made frequent voyages back and forth between Molfetta and various points on the Adriatic. During these trips we touched at all the principal ports of Italy and Dalmatia; Brindisi, Bari, Foggia, Ancona, Ravenna, Venice, Triest, Pola, Fiume, Zara, Sebenico, and others. Some of these spots are enshrined in natural grandeur all-surpassing. The very sight of them brought profound satisfaction and left lasting imprints upon the retina of my mind's eye. But soon I had seen "all the world" on the Adriatic, and my gaze began to turn toward other and wider horizons. "For it's 'all day' with you when you answer the cue" says Robert Service. Other worlds were calling, and I heeded the call.

Meanwhile, mother, father and dear grandmother

had all died. Some one was unkind enough to say that it was because of pain, pain over my "impertinenza," that they had gone. My child eyes stared in amazement; I wondered if this was so. However, the fact was that grandmother died of age—she was over 85—while both father and mother had died in the midst of a strenuous effort to save their children from a scarlet fever epidemic which swept over Molfetta and carried away many of its inhabitants. Our home was broken up, the girls soon afterward married, while the three other boys were taken over by relatives.

And now securing permission from Uncle Carlo, who had been appointed our legal guardian, I set out upon paths which led to more distant lands. He loaned me fifty *lire*, and two days after Christmas in 1899, I started for Genoa, the leading seaport of Italy. There I embarked on board merchant ships, mainly steamers, and for over a year I made voyages to different parts of Europe. We went to Alexandria, but I do not even remember how the city looked. Of Greece I remember the charm of the Ægean Islands and Athens, slumbering in the peace of centuries. Of Constantinople I recall the majesty of St. Sophia, the squalor of the sordid streets and the enchanting beauty of the city of minarets reflected in the tranquil waters of the Sea of Marmora. The very name "the Black Sea" brings back the memory of black, ugly clouds hovering low like vultures upon the darksome waters. Of the Danube I can only remember its muddy color and the enormous river barges dragged by mules along the shore. Roumania brings back the picture of ancient villages and of women loading the steamer with enormous baskets of grain which they carried upon their heads, all the while puffing at huge pipes. Wales brings to my ear the plaintive songs of the Welsh, while Edinburgh brings to mind the dense fogs, the ugliness of its down-town streets and my first sight of ice covering a body of water.

While visiting these various European countries, my eyes had often turned longingly toward the west, to the continent beyond the setting sun, on the other side of the great Atlantic. Some day I was going to see America. At last my opportunity came. In Genoa I heard of a new brig, the *Francesco*, which was to make her maiden voyage to America, Australia, the South Sea Islands and thence through the Suez Canal back to Genoa, her starting point. The voyage was to last about thirty months. I sought and secured a place on her crew, with the thought that at the end of this voyage I would return to Molfetta and settle down for the rest of my life. Destiny, however, had decreed otherwise. On a day not far-distant, without even dreaming of it, I was to become a part of America.

It will doubtless be of interest to the reader to see the picture which I had of America as I

turned my face westward. It is generally supposed that immigrants, as they turn their steps toward America, have a true idea of what the country
is like, its life, its institutions, its natural resources
and beauty. How true this is will appear from the
picture of America which follows. This is all the
more significant because I had lived my childhood in
an immediate environment where education was the
rule. I had also come in contact with persons who
had traveled widely, particulaily my seafaring uncle,
and it would seem that I ought to have had a true
mental picture of America.

Of course, like every Italian boy, I had heard
from earliest childhood of America, the continent
which "Colombo," one of our countrymen, had long
ago discovered. However, my idea of America was
as misty as that of the Old World on the day when
Columbus returned from his famous voyage. Rubbing its eyes and stretching out its arms as if
awakening from a sleep of centuries, it began to
realize that a new day had dawned in the history
of mankind. We used to sing a song; it was about
thirty stanzas long, and it told all the story of that
famous voyage, but it had nothing in it about the
continent he had found, or what was on that continent in our day. Like every boy who goes through
the third grade of Italian schools, I had read the
story of America in De Amici's famous book, "Il
Cuore." But while that story, "From the Appe-

nines to the Andes" is one of unexcelled imaginative beauty, it gives little or no details of the country beyond the setting sun, of its people, its institutions, its life in general. Moreover, that story deals with South America rather than North America.

Now that is one point of interest in the picture I had of America in my childhood; to me there was no distinction between North and South America. There was but one America. I had read something of Boston and New York, but the words brought only a vague and indefinite idea to my mind. Even Montevideo and Buenos Ayres, of which I had heard much, were far from definite and concrete realities. Two things alone I seemed able to picture; the vast stretches of virgin lands and the great, winding rivers. I had read something of the Indians, who were very much like the cannibals of my childhood stories. The uncle to whom I have already referred would often recount stories of his voyages to America, but these presented vague pictures and were invariably connected with thrilling experiences with pirates which he had had off the coast of that continent. Such persons as had emigrated from Molfetta had usually gone to South America, and when they returned, they told stories of the money they had made rather than giving descriptions of the country and its people. I remember only one person whom I ever heard say anything

about the country itself; a man who had worked as
cook on board a barge at Rio de Janeiro. He was
wont to wax eloquent about the beauty of the country, the leisureliness of the people, the majesty of
great rivers and the mildness of the climate. He
also, however, spoke principally of the money he
had made.

I knew of only one person who had gone from
our small city to North America. He came to visit
Molfetta when I was a small boy, and his visit left
certain distinct impressions upon my mind. He had
lived in America for several years. From what I
recall, it seems that he had changed his name while
living in America, and therefore his family had
lost all trace of him, and considered him dead. They
were friends of our family, and when he finally
came back for a visit, I was much impressed. I remember him as clearly as if it were to-day. He
could not speak our dialect any more. What little
of the language he spoke was the pure Italian,
which he had learned in America. I recall also his
purple, showy necktie, and a stickpin with bril-
liants. What impressed me most of all was the
white collar which he wore. These things were great
luxuries in our town, worn only by the well-to-do,
and not by "la gente," or common folks, to which he
belonged.

Another close-up view of America which I got
in my childhood was that of what I thought were

American sailors on board an American steamer, which chanced to come to Molfetta. This was such a rare happening that of course I learned of it, and taking a special leave of absence from school, I went to call upon the honorable gentlemen, the American sailors. For all I know they may have been Chinese coolies, but as long as they were on board an American steamer, to me they were Americans. There were several interesting and peculiar things about these American sailors. For one thing, they were very paragons of filth. I liked to hear them speak their foreign, and to me, "barbarian" language. I can recall to-day their shouts as they unloaded the coal. And most interesting of all was the sight of them drunk on the streets of our little Molfetta, where drunken persons were never seen. They had gone ashore, and taking advantage of the inexpensiveness of our good Molfettese wine, they had laid in a goodly provision of it, and from the way they staggered about the streets, it was evident that they had stored away within their bodily cellars slightly more than they could carry well. We boys followed them from street to street, and made sport of them in order to hear their funny jabbering.

Another glimpse of America, strangely contradictory to the one I have just related, came through a ship builder who lived in Molfetta. This man was quite well-to-do, and greatly respected in our town. He had been in America several years, had

AMERICA

63

made money and returned to our city, where he
had established a shipbuilding business of his own.
He was, however, considered one of the queerest
and most extraordinary members of our little society, for the reason that he did not drink wine or
liquors of any kind. Some people had been skepti-
cal about the truth of this report, but professional
gossipers had made a careful investigation and it
was now generally accepted that this man, the
strangest human being in our town, actually did
not drink wine, even the light white wines for which
Molfetta was famous. It was understood that he
had acquired this freakish habit in America.   Of
course, in my childhood days I did not see the connection between drunkenness of the American sailors
on the one hand and the total abstinence of this man
from liquors on the other.

Still another view of America had come to me
through the eyes of a blind man. In my boyhood,
he was a man of about fifty years of age; stone
blind, and led about the streets by a small boy. The
story was that he had been in America, where he
had worked "in campagna"—in the country—and
that the climate was so hot that he had lost his eye-
sight by sun-stroke. He had been back in Molfetta
for some twenty years. Apparently he had made
some money before his return, for he did not seem
to be a mendicant like most of the blind people of
the town. To me the most striking thing about

this man was that he was the only person in
Molfetta who could speak English, and he always
acted as interpreter when English or American ves-
sels chanced to come to the city. It was this man
who first awakened in me a desire to learn the English language. I used to think that if I could learn
English and become an "interrupter" myself, I
would be in the height of my glory.

From some source I got the idea that America
was a continent of great forests, and that the trees
when cut grew again, not new trees, but that they
grew up again from the stumps, and that by this
method of growth America was always covered with
great stretches of forests.

Now it does not require a great artist nor a
great stretch of the imagination to piece together
these various fragments and create a picture of
America as I saw it when I turned my steps westward; it was a great country, vast in its propor-
tions, vaguely beautiful, covered with forests, leis-
urely-winding rivers and great stretches of farm
lands. There were some large cities like Montevideo or Boston, a little larger perhaps than Genoa,
or Naples, and all belonging to the same country. It
was so hot that persons working in the fields became
blind from sunstroke. In that country lived many
pirates who attacked passing ships; dirty drunken
sailors who spoke a barbarian tongue; the Indians,
who were a sort of wild creatures on the order of

cannibals. People from Molfetta went there and made much money. Some of them acquired strange habits, like not drinking wine or not speaking our dialect any more, wearing white collars and purple neckties when they belonged to the "gente."

Far be it from me to say that this is the mental picture which all Italians have as they turn their faces toward America. Far be it from the reader to take it as seriously as a certain popular writer recently did when he suggested that, because Italians have such a picture as this of America, they should be barred from entering this country. I only give it as *my* picture of America. I knew nothing of its people, its government, its institutions, its vastness and greatness. Soon, however, I was to be enriched and enlightened in ways I had not dreamed. For what is true of America is true of all countries; no far-off glimpse can give a correct picture of their peoples or institutions, and only as a person learns to know them intimately is he able to measure them in terms of real values.

IN THE AMERICAN STORM

Not that they starve, but starve so dreamlessly,
Not that they sow, but that they seldom reap,
Not that they serve, but have no gods to serve,
Not that they die, but that they die like sheep.
Vachel Lindsay.

CHAPTER IV

T HE *Francesco* put out to sea from Trapani,
Sicily, on May 3, 1902, and a week or so later
passed the Pillars of Hercules. Then she
plunged into the wake of the trade winds and for
about three weeks she sailed majestically before them
like a gull, stirring not a sail all the while. Then followed a period of varying weather, which in turn was
succeeded by a few days when the ocean was breathless and motionless. Frequently we could see whole
schools of dolphins as they came to the surface,
or monster whales spurting pillars of water into the
air, a sight especially beautiful on calm moonlit
nights.

The little brig had reached a distance of about
three hundred miles from the coast of North America, when one day the very weight of heaven seemed
to be pressing down upon her. The clouds were
yellow, sullen and angry-looking; the air was
breathless with pent-up power. As the day advanced
the barometer went lower and lower, and with the
approach of evening this invisible, uncontrollable

power seemed to be seizing the little ship as if with mighty claws. The sea rumbled beneath her, the thick masses of clouds pressed closer upon her, the waters became deep-dyed black. At five-thirty we heard the call: "All hands on deck," and a few moments later: "All sails in but lower-topsail and jib." Climbing like monkeys after coconuts, we made short work of the task. We knew, however, that something more strenuous was coming. At six, just as the four bells were striking, the very bowels of sea and sky opened upon us with amazing suddenness and force. The seasoned Tuscan sailor, whose every word was wont to be an oath, struck with sudden fear, fell upon his knees by the bulwark and began to say his prayers. Some one kicked him as you would a dog. The moment the terrific gale struck the ship it tore the heavy lower-top-sail and flapped it madly in the air as if it were a piece of tissue paper. The brave little ship bent pitifully beneath the gale; its mainroyalmast was broken like a reed; its cargo was shifted to one side like a handful of pebbles, and its hull sprung a leak. The blast was over in an hour or so, but all hands worked steadily for three days and nights to shift the cargo back in place, while four men were kept at the hand-pump night and day until we reached shore a week or more later.

Some years afterward an American friend, reflecting upon this incident as I had described it to him, remarked "That storm was indeed prophetic of your early experiences in America, was it not?" It may be that it was, and perhaps we shall soon discover the analogy as it appeared in my friend's mind.

On July 3rd, 1902, after a voyage of sixty-one day, the *Francesco* anchored in Boston Harbor. As the next day was the "Fourth," the city was already decked in festal array. The captain hastened to register his arrival. A boat was lowered, and I was ordered to take him ashore; thus it was my good fortune to be the first to touch land. "America!" I whispered to myself as I did so.

In a day or two the ship was towed to a pier in Charlestown, where it lay until its cargo of salt was unloaded and a cargo of lumber consigned to Montevideo was put on board of her.

In the meantime a desire had arisen within me to return home. There were several reasons for this. In the first place, it was becoming increasingly unpleasant for me to remain in the midst of that crew. It chanced that I was the only person on board hailing from southern Italy; the rest of the men were mostly Genoese, with one or two Tuscans. Now, the feeling of sectional provincialism between north and south Italy is still so strong, and the North always assumes such airs of superiority, that I had become the butt of every joke and the scapegoat of every occasion. This was becoming more and more unbearable, and as time went on I decided that my self-respect could not and would not stand it. To this was added the fact that the captain was one of those creatures who seem to be more brute than man, especially in dealing with youth. During that voyage he had more than once beaten me in a way that would have made the hardest punishments of my father blush. He was so cruel and unreasonable that before he left Boston several of the crew, including the first mate, left him.

In the face of these circumstances I began to think that if the captain would only let me go, I would return home. Accordingly, one day I went to him and very respectfully told him of my intention to return to Italy immediately if he would permit me, and would pay me the money which was due me. The stern, sea-hardened sailor brushed me aside without even an answer. A day or so later I again went to him; this time he drove me from his presence with a sharp kick. Whatever manhood there ever was in my being rose up and stood erect within me; with a determination as quick and as sharp as his kick had been, I decided I would now go at any cost.

I began to look about for ways and means to carry out my determination. On the pier was an elderly watchman, an Italian by birth, who had been in America for several years. To him I confided my difficulties. He was a sane and conserv-

ative man, cautious in giving advice. My desire was
to find a ship which was returning to some European port. He did not know of any, but one evening he suggested that if worse came to worst, I
could do some kind of work for a few days and
thereby earn enough money to buy a third-class
passage back to Naples, which at that time cost
only fifty or sixty dollars. This gave me a new
idea. I decided to take my destiny in my own
hands and in some way find my way back to
Italy. Two months had already passed since our
arrival in Boston, and almost any day now the vessel would take to sea. If I were to act it must be
now or never. I had been ashore twice and had
become acquainted with a barber near the pier. To
him I also confided my troubles, and he offered to
keep my few belongings for me, should I finally decide to leave the ship.

Late in the evening of September 8, 1902, when
the turmoil of the street traffic was subsiding, and
the silence of the night was slowly creeping over
the city, I took my sea chest, my sailor bag and
all I had and set foot on American soil. I was in
America. Of immigration laws I had not even a
knowledge of their existence; of the English language I knew not a word; of friends I had none
in Boston or elsewhere in America to whom I might
turn for counsel or help. I had exactly fifty cents
remaining out of a dollar which the captain had

finally seen fit to give me. But as I was soon to earn money and return to Molfetta, I felt no concern.

My Charlestown barber friend took me in that first night with the distinct understanding that I could stay only one night. So the next morning bright and early, leaving all my belongings with the barber, I started out in search of a job. I roamed about the streets, not knowing where or to whom to turn. That day and the next four days I had one loaf of bread each day for food and at night, not having money with which to purchase shelter, I stayed on the recreation pier on Commercial Street. One night, very weary and lonely, I lay upon a bench and soon dozed off into a light sleep. The next thing I knew I cried out in bitter pain and fright. A policeman had stolen up to me very quietly and with his club had dealt me a heavy blow upon the soles of my feet. He drove me away, and I think I cried; I cried my first American cry. What became of me that night I cannot say. And the next day and the next. . . . I just roamed aimlessly about the streets, between the Public Garden with its flowers and the water-side, where I watched the children at play, even as I had played at the water's brink in old Molfetta.

Those first five days in America have left an impression upon my mind which can never be erased with the years, and which gives me a most profound sense of sympathy for immigrants as they arrive.

On the fifth day, by mere chance, I ran across a French sailor on the recreation pier. We immediately became friends. His name was Louis. Just to look at Louis would make you laugh. He was over six feet tall, lank, queer-shaped, freckle-faced, with small eyes and a crooked nose. I have sometimes thought that perhaps he was the "missing link" for which the scientist has been looking. Louis could not speak Italian; he had a smattering of what he called "italien," but I could not see it his way. On the other hand, I kept imposing upon his good nature by giving a nasal twang to Italian words and insisting on calling it "francese." We had much merriment. Two facts, however, made possible a mutual understanding. Both had been sailors and had traveled over very much the same world; this made a bond between us. Then too, we had an instinctive knowledge of "esperanto," a strange capacity for gesticulation and facial contortion, which was always our last "hope" in making each other understand.

Not far from the recreation pier on which we met is located the Italian colony of "North End," Boston. To this Louis and I made our way, and to an Italian boarding house. How we happened to find it and to get in I do not now recall. It was a "three-room apartment" and the landlady informed us that she was already "full," but since we had no place to go, she would take us in. Added to the host that was already gathered there, our coming made fourteen people. At night the floor of the kitchen and the dining table were turned into beds. Louis and I were put to sleep in one of the beds with two other men, two facing north and two south. As I had slept all my life in a bed or bunk by myself this quadrupling did not appeal to me especially. But we could not complain. We had been taken in on trust, and the filth, the smells and the crowding together were a part of the trust.

We began to make inquiries about jobs and were promptly informed that there was plenty of work at "pick and shovel." We were also given to understand by our fellow-boarders that "pick and shovel" was practically the only work available to Italians. Now these were the first two English words I had heard and they possessed great charm. Moreover, if I were to earn money to return home and this was the only work available for Italians, they were very weighty words for me, and I must master them as soon and as well as possible and then set out to find their hidden meaning. I practised for a day or two until I could say "peek" and "shuvle" to perfection. Then I asked a fellow-boarder to take me to see what the work was like. He did. He led me to Washington Street, not far from the colony, where some excavation work was going on, and there I did see, with my own eyes, what the "peek" and "shuvle" were about. My heart sank within me,

for I had thought it some form of office work; but
I was game and since this was the only work available for Italians, and since I must have money to
return home, I would take it up. After all, it was
only a means to an end, and would last but a few
days.

It may be in place here to say a word relative to
the reason why this idea was prevalent among Italians at the time, and why so many Italians on coming to America find their way to what I had called
"peek and shuvle." It is a matter of common
knowledge, at least among students of immigration,
that a very large percentage of Italian immigrants
were "contadini" or farm laborers in Italy. American people often ask the question, "Why do they not
go to the farms in this country?" This query is
based upon the idea that the "contadini" were farmers in the sense in which we apply that word to the
American farmer. The facts in the case are that
the "contadini" were not farmers in that sense at
all, but simply farm-laborers, more nearly serfs,
working on landed estates and seldom owning their
own land. Moreover, they are not in any way acquainted with the implements of modern American
farming. Their farming tools consisted generally
of a "zappa," a sort of wide mattock; an ax and
the wooden plow of biblical times. When they come
to America, the work which comes nearest to that
which they did in Italy is not farming, or even farm

labor, but excavation work. This fact, together with the isolation which inevitably would be their's on an American farm, explains, in a large measure, why so few Italians go to the farm and why so many go into excavation work. There is another factor to be considered, and that is that the "padrone" perhaps makes a greater per capita percentage in connection with securing and managing workers for construction purposes than in any other line, and therefore he becomes a walking delegate about the streets of Italian colonies spreading the word that only "peek and shuvle" is available.

Now, though Louis and I had never done such work, because we were Italians we must needs adapt ourselves to it and go to work with "peek and shuvle." (I should have stated that Louis, desiring to be like the Romans while living with them, for the time being passed for an Italian.)

So we went out to hunt our first job in America. For several mornings Louis and I went to North Square, where there were generally a large number of men loitering in groups discussing all kinds of subjects, particularly the labor market. One morning we were standing in front of one of those infernal institutions which in America are permitted to bear the name of "immigrant banks," when we saw a fat man coming toward us. "Buon giorno, padrone," said one of the men. "Padrone?" said I to myself. Now the word "padrone" in Italy is applied to a proprietor, generally a respectable man, at least one whose dress and appearance distinguish him as a man of means. This man not only showed no signs of good breeding in his face, but he was unshaven and dirty and his clothes were shabby. I could not quite understand how he could be called "padrone." However, I said nothing, first because I wanted to get back home, and second because I wanted to be polite when I was in *American* society!

The "padrone" came up to our group and began tò wax eloquent and to gesticulate (both in Sicilian dialect) about the advantages of a certain job. I remember very clearly the points which he emphasized: "It is not very far, only twelve miles from Boston. For a few cents you can come back any time you wish, to see 'i parenti e gli amici,' your relatives and friends. The company has a 'shantee' in which you can sleep, and a 'storo' where you can buy your 'grosserie' all very cheap. 'Buona paga'," he continued "(Good pay), $1.25 per day, and you only have to pay me fifty cents a week for having gotten you this 'gooda jobba.' I only do it to help you and because you are my countrymen. If you come back here at six o'clock to-night with your bundles, I myself will take you out."

The magnanimity of this man impressed Louis and me very profoundly; we looked at each other and said, "Wonderful!" We decided we would go;

so at the appointed hour we returned to the very spot. About twenty men finally gathered there and we were led to North Station. There we took a train to some suburban place, the name of which I have never been able to learn. On reaching our destination we were taken to the "shantee" where we were introduced to two long open bunks filled with straw. These were to be our beds. The "storo" of which we had been told was at one end of the shanty. The next morning we were taken out to work. It was a sultry autumn day. The "peek" seemed to grow heavier at every stroke and the "shuvle" wider and larger in its capacity to hold the gravel. The second day was no better than the first, and the third was worse than the second. The work was heavy and monotonous to Louis and myself especially, who had never been "contadini" like the rest. The "padrone" whose magnanimity had so stirred us was little better than a brute. We began to do some simple figuring and discovered that when we had paid for our groceries at the "storo," for the privilege of sleeping in the shanty, and the fifty cents to the "padrone" for having been so condescending as to employ us, we would have nothing left but sore arms and backs. So on the afternoon of the third day Louis and I held a solemn conclave and decided to part company with "peek and shuvle,"—for ever. We left, without receiving a cent of pay, of course.

Going across country on foot we came to a small manufacturing village. We decided to try our luck at the factory, which proved to be a woolen mill, and found employment. Our work was sorting old rags and carrying them in wheelbarrows into a hot oven, in which the air was almost suffocating. Every time a person went in it he was obliged to run out as quickly as possible, for the heat was unbearable. Unfortunately for us, the crew was composed almost entirely of Russians, who hated us from the first day, and called us "dagoes." I had never heard the word before; I asked Louis if he knew its meaning, but he did not. In going in and out of the oven the Russians would crowd against us and make it hard for us to pass. One morning as I was coming out, four of the men hedged me in. I thought I would suffocate. I finally succeeded in pushing out, my hand having been cut in the rush of the wheelbarrows.

The superintendent of the factory had observed the whole incident. He was a very kindly man. From his light complexion I think he was a Swede. He came to my rescue, reprimanded the Russians, and led me to his office, where he bandaged my hand. Then he called Louis and explained the situation to us. The Russians looked upon us as intruders and were determined not to work side by side with "the foreigners," but to drive them out of the factory. Therefore, much as he regretted it, the superintendent was obliged to ask us to leave, since there were only two of us, as against the large number of Russians who made up his unskilled crew.

So we left. My bandaged hand hurt me, but my heart hurt more. This kind of work was hard and humiliating enough, but what went deeper than all else was the first realization that because of race I was being put on the road. And often since that day have I felt the cutting thrusts of race prejudice. They have been dealt by older immigrants, who are known as "Americans," as well as by more recent comers. All have been equally heart-rending and head-bending. I hold no grudge against any one; I realize that it is one of the attendant circumstances of our present nationalistic attitude the world over, and yet it is none the less saddening to the human heart. I have seen prejudice, like an evil shadow, everywhere. It lurks at every corner, on every street and in every mart. I have seen it in the tram and on the train; I have felt its dreaded power in school and college, in clubs and churches. It is an ever-present evil spirit, felt though unseen, wounding hearts, cutting souls. It passes on its poison like a serpent from generation to generation, and he who would see the fusion of the various elements into a truly American type must ever take into cognizance its presence in the hearts of some human beings.

We had to hunt another job. We returned to

Boston still penniless and to the good graces of the "padrona" of the filthy boarding-house. Louis now spent a penny for an Italian newspaper and looked over the "want ads." He saw what seemed to be a good prospect for a job and we decided to apply for it. If you walk down lower Washington Street in Boston, toward North Station, facing the Italian colony, near Hanover Street you can see, even now, a large sign, "Stobhom Employment Agency." It is a notorious institution, the function of which is to catch men and send them to a company in Bangor, from which place they are sent to the various camps in the woods of Maine.

We called upon said "honorable" agency and were told that they could supply us with work. "It is out in the country, in the woods of Maine. Wages $30 per month, board and room. Good, healthy job." It sounded too good to let go, so we accepted the offer. We were told to report that night at seven o'clock and we would be directed to our work. These night meetings seem to be quite popular with such agencies! Now, I knew what the country was like, but I had no idea what "woods" meant, and with the best of Louis' wretched Italian, I couldn't quite get it through my head. Moreover, Maine might be anywhere from North Boston to California for all I knew. However, we decided to try it. At $30 per month I would only need to work two months at most; then back home for me!

We reported at seven o'clock according to instructions. A crowd of men jammed the office, the stairway, and loitered on the sidewalk—a whole regiment, all properly equipped with their personal belongings. I had my sea-chest and small sailor bag which Louis helped me to carry. At about nine o'clock the exodus began. We were led to North Station and huddled together three deep in one car. The train soon pulled out and I went to "bed," which consisted of the arm of a seat. The filth, the smoke, the sights of that memorable trip come back to me as I write by the midnight candle. We traveled all that night and the next day, with nothing to eat except what little food each man had brought with him. At two o'clock the next afternoon we reached our destination. The station was of the kind often seen in the unsettled regions of America—a small shack put up by the side of the railroad tracks, where perhaps a hunter unloaded his pack once; properly propped up, lest the winds some night should steal it away; with a sign placed upon it, thus giving it the dignified name of "station." The name of this station was Norcross.

The starving multitude emerged from the "special car" on short notice. We followed the "boss" to a small steamer about thirty-five feet long. Ordinarily it would not have carried over fifty people, but it took practically all of us. In spite of my sea-loving instincts, my heart sank within me. But as we were promised food as soon as we had crossed the lake, Louis and I pushed our way in, my chest and bag dragging behind. It was dark by the time we reached the upper end of one of the Twin Lakes. We landed in the heart of a solitary forest. I knew then what a "woods" was. As soon as we were all on "terra foresta" we smelled food, and then and there I had my first taste of pork and beans, molasses cookies and coffee and "cream." Soon after eating we "turned in," with the starry heavens above us and pine needles pricking beneath, we rested our weary bodies.

The next morning we began our "boring in" process. The opening up of a new lumbering camp generally follows on this wise: First, the land is surveyed; main and side roads are opened; bridges are built over brooks and marshy places; stumps are blown up; wayside houses are erected for provisions and horses, and a number of other preliminary things are done before the final camp is set up. We were set to perform these preliminary tasks.

I was given an ax and a whetstone. As I was a seaman and had never wielded such weapons before, at first I was at sea to know what to do with them. But imitating others, I tried my hand at it, but soon found my ax handle-less. I seemed to have the knack of hitting the tree once and only once in the same place. No one dared work within a radius of twenty yards of me for fear of losing his life. The boss, who was a Scandinavian, was very patient and kind, and seeing my lack of skill at chopping trees, put me to work dragging small logs into the paths for the men who were building bridges. But I was equally as untrained in the art of being a mule as I was unskilled in wielding an ax. It strained my back and I "kicked." At last I was placed at "fetching" water for the lumbermen, thirsty creatures that they were, who took one drink of water to every two strokes of the ax. So even "fetching water" was no mean task.

One day while hunting for a new brook I had an awful fright. I heard the breaking of boughs and saw, or thought I saw, a wild animal. As a child, my family used to frighten me into obedience by saying, "A wild beast will get you." Now all my fear came back and a chill of terror seized me. Using my shinning ability to its nth power, on very short notice I was up a tree and there they found me at night. The bucket at the foot of the tree was the only sign of my whereabouts. That same night I lost a black-handled pocket knife, an heirloom, belonging originally to my maternal grandfather, who was drowned at sea. As something very mysterious happened later in connection with this knife, it will be of interest to remember it.

We were nine days in building bridges and opening roads before we reached the location of our permanent camp. Our food was changed daily from pork and beans, molasses cookies and coffee and "cream"—to coffee and "cream," molasses cookies and pork and beans, with some pea soup added for good measure.

In the meantime, I had begun to nave some mighty strong convictions that Louis and I had better emerge from this existence. So we held a secret Italo-French diplomatic conference and on the evening of the ninth day we packed up our belongings and left the camp. Of course, we drew no pay.

We traveled all night and most of the next day before we reached the "wayside house" by the lake, where we had first landed. The next morning the little steamer which had brought us to the spot came up and we requested the captain to take us across. He flatly refused, saying that we had come there to work, not to go back; and steaming up he disappeared. I learned years afterwards that this was not simply an incident in my life, but a part of a system known as "peonage." Men, mostly of foreign birth, are taken to these lumber camps. surrounded by some kind of barrier which makes escape impossible, and there they are compelled to remain. According to United States Government reports, there are thousands, mostly Scandinavians and Slavs, in the lumbering regions of our country, who are trapped in some such way and often compelled to work in this form of slavery sometimes for months. The barrier in our case consisted of virgin forests on three sides and a large body of water on the other.

However, Louis and I did not intend to be caught, and our sailor's ingenuity now stood us in good stead. We dragged a few logs together and tied them into a raft with ropes and chains which we found on the shore; we made some poles to push the raft and placing our belongings upon it, toward sunset of the second day we started on our famous journey. For food we filled two whisky bottles with molasses from a barrel which we found on shore.

We had scarcely pushed off when we heard shouting. I immediately thought of the "wild Indians" of my childhood stories. It proved to be a Russian who also had left the camp. He waved his ax in the air and entreated us to come back to shore. From his gesticulation and facial contortions, it became clear to us that he meant no harm, but that all he wanted was a free passage on our new "trans-lake-anic" liner! We pulled back to shore, took him on and started again upon our way. The harmony which followed can be better imagined than described. With a Russian, a Frenchman and an Italian, each not understanding the other, we and our tongues were repeatedly and completely confounded and we had a twentieth century "Tower of Babel" on a raft on an American lake.

We pushed away from shore and started on our journey toward the unknown. We knew nothing of our whereabouts and depended solely on our general sense of direction. Toward dusk we reached the other side of an inlet not far from the starting-point, and the question now came up as to what we should do during the night. Naturally there was not much discussion about the matter simply because the linguistic facilities for discussion were totally absent. We pulled ashore, however, and from the preparations which Louis and our Russian "comrade" began to make, I could see that we were destined to put up here for the night. While the last faint gleams of light were disappearing, we gathered a few sticks of wood, (the Russian's ax coming in handy for this purpose), and built a fire.

It was one of those autumn nights when the penetrating chill of the air seems to creep to the very marrow of one's bones. The sky was overhung with thick clouds like omens foreboding ill. Not a star was to be seen. The wind made a mournful sound through the tree-tops. And in the thick darkness the glare of the fire cast pale and fitful shadows. Louis and the Russian were soon fast asleep. A creeping fear began to steal over me. Through the forest I could hear the cries of wild animals, and from afar came the mournful low of the moose and the deer. With every gust of wind a chill of terror swept over me and it seemed as if I could see animals coming toward me. Once in my frenzy I cried out at the top of my voice and shook Louis out of his deep slumber. He assured me that no animal would come near as long as the fire was burning. But this was poor consolation for the pile of wood was fast dwindling, and if the fire was to be kept burning, I must go to the forest and gather more. I implored Louis to stay awake with me, but he turned over and was soon asleep again. I managed to gather more wood and all night long I kept the fire burning. Perhaps the reader can imagine in some measure what went through my mind that night. I cannot describe it.

With the first streak of dawn, I woke my companions and insisted on leaving at once the spot where I had spent such a night of misery, and on continuing our journey. We boarded our raft and were soon pushing our way along in the shallow waters. Toward noon we heard the blowing of a whistle. At this, the Russian made motions indicating that we should abandon the raft and strike across the forest in the direction from which the sound of the whistle came. Louis was inclined to follow his proposal, but for me it was not such a simple matter. On that raft were all my earthly possessions, not much, I grant you, but in that sea

chest and sailor bag were all that was left to remind
me of home and loved ones. Louis finally decided to
follow our Russian friend through the woods. He
had gone a few paces when I was seized with a
sudden determination that he must not leave me
alone in these wilds. He had been partly responsible for my coming to this forsaken country; he had
agreed to leave the camp with me and attempt to
escape from the trap in which we had been caught,
and he must stay with me and see the game through,
at all costs. I picked up a rock and marched up to
Louis. He did not understand what I said with my
tongue, but he understood perfectly well what I was
saying with the rock in my hand. Although Louis
was nearly twice my size, he was a moral coward.
He offered no resistance, and waving good-by to
the Russian, went back to the raft with me. That
was the last we saw of our Russian friend, and we
never learned whether he found his way out of the
forest.

Louis and I again boarded the raft and pushed
our way along the shore. By evening we were beginning to get very hungry. The two bottles of
molasses were almost exhausted. Above everything else, I feared another night in those desolate
wilds; and we had no ax with which to get wood.
Just then in the glow of the sunset rays we saw
a column of smoke. Have you ever been out at
sea or in a forest and roamed for days not knowing

your bearings, and all at once out of the unknown comes some sign that help is near, and your sinking heart gives a leap of courage? That was the feeling that now came over us. But we must act quickly. If we would not spend another night in the dreaded woods we must make an immediate dash toward the smoke. We dragged the raft onto a promontory, buried my belongings under a pile of rock and started on our quest of life. As I looked back upon that pile of rocks, it seemed as if I was leaving the dearest friends I had on earth. But I had no choice—I must go or starve in that wild forest.

We began to climb over dead trees and through the underbrush, making very slow progress. Here and there we found marshy spots over which we had to go carefully or be sucked into the soft, spongy ground beneath our feet. Meantime it was getting darker and darker. For a time we feared we would never reach our destination; the thought even crossed my mind that we would fall exhausted and be eaten by wild beasts. But we kept on, perspiring and breathless, but driven by desperation.

After struggling for an hour or so, we came out near the spot where we had seen smoke rising, and we heard the sound of human voices. We drew near and saw that it was a sort of floating cabin or houseboat. It was really a floating lumber camp. At first we were afraid to go in, fearing it might be a part of the same establishment from which we had escaped, and we would be caught again. But as it was a matter of life and death, we plucked up our courage and went on, first concealing what was left of our molasses. As we approached the raft, we smelled food. The crew was eating supper. When we appeared at the door there was a general commotion within; the lumbermen did not know what to make of these strange creatures. Louis did what he could to explain our predicament, and they immediately offered us the hospitality of the camp. We ate a sumptuous supper and then Louis told at length the story of our escape. We were given a place to sleep on the floor, which seemed as soft as down to our weary bodies.

We learned next morning that this was a rival camp to the one from which we had escaped. The boss was "horrified" at the treatment we had received, and assumed the attitude of a protector and a defender of justice. We told him how we had left my belongings under the rocks on the promontory and he loaned us a boat to go after them, making sure that we would not escape with the boat, by sending two men along with us. We brought back my sea chest and bag to the camp and that night the lumber jacks had an enjoyable entertainment looking over the strange things contained in them.

Some little trinkets I gave away to the men in token of appreciation of the kindness they had shown us; other articles disappeared mysteriously.

On the following morning the boss hailed the steamer as it passed by, and after much argument forced the captain, who three days before had refused us passage, to take us to Norcross. Once on board, the captain demanded the payment of twelve dollars for our passage. We told him we had no money and showed him the inside of our pockets. He agreed to land us at Norcross provided we would leave my belongings until we could come back to pay him the money. It was not until months afterward that I was able to redeem them.

We emerged from this camp only to find our way to another, as there was no other work available in the vicinity. It was while in this second camp that I came near losing my life. It was now late October. The snows were beginning to fall, adorning the trees with matchless white and making a thin crust of ice over rivers and lakes. Such spotless beauty I had never seen before; the whole scene was enchanting to me. In all my life I had seen snow only once, and at Edinburgh I had once seen ice covering the water.

One day I was detailed to go on an errand to Millinocket, some five miles away, across the river. To cross the river one might follow one of two courses, either go down to the bridge, some three miles down-stream, or cross over the rocks at a narrow place, which was fairly passable when the river was low. On reaching the river I decided to take the latter course. My father had taught me that a straight line is the shortest distance between two points. So it is in the abstract. But unfortunately it did not prove to be so in this case. I noticed that the waters were gushing over the narrows and that it was impossible to cross at that point. Not far down-stream, however, I saw a man crossing on the ice. The sight fascinated me; in my childhood I had dreamed of walking on the water, and now it seemed that my dream would actually come true. Without a moment's hesitation I chose what I thought a convenient place to cross and began to make my way. Some two or three miles above Millinocket the Penobscot River passes through a narrow ravine and then broadens majestically as it approaches the gigantic falls which furnish power for one of the greatest pulp mills in the world. I chose a comparatively narrow place to cross, having no way of knowing that waters run swiftest in the narrows. As I made my way toward the middle of the river I noticed that the ice was not so white as near the edge, but did not connect it with any possible weakness in the smooth and beautiful pavement under me. I walked slowly in order not to slip. I had reached the middle of the river, when of a sudden, without warning, the ice broke under my feet and I went down into the icy and swiftly moving current.

For the next fifteen minutes I had a battle for life. The madly-rushing waters dragged my feet under the thin layer of ice. I would get hold of the edge of the frail substance only to find it breaking in my hand while I struggled to get a firmer grasp. I lay flat on the ice, thinking I could thus distribute my weight, but whole pieces would break under me and I would be floating on a large piece of thin ice. How I finally managed to crawl to shore I cannot say. My clothing was soon frozen stiff in the chill wind and I was completely exhausted. It was not until the next day that I fully regained consciousness and realized all that had happened. I was then in my bunk at the camp. It appears that some one had picked me up and carried me back to camp. I never understood the details. Truly this was a "cool" reception which Monsieur North America was giving to a son of Sunny Italy.

All through that winter I suffered greatly from the cold and I did not know what it was to be really comfortable. Sometimes when I hear people speaking rather disparagingly of immigrants from temperate climates for hibernating during the cold winter months, I am reminded of the experiences of

the first winter in North America and I understand
fully why these humble peasants of sunny climes are
willing to work all the harder in the summer months
in order not to be exposed to the rigors of the
winter.

So climatic conditions indirectly become no small
factor in the assimilation of certain immigrant
groups and the non-assimilation of others.   The
crisp cold that puts a spring in the steps of some
drives others to cover.   Were it possible to properly
distribute these people according to the climatic
conditions of the different parts of the country it
would be otherwise; however, that question cannot
be considered here.   Climate also explains in a
measure why so many immigrants return to their
native land from year to year.

It was about this time that Louis and I came to
the parting of the ways.   We had come to work in
still another logging camp, the crew of which was
made up entirely of French Canadians.   Louis felt
very much at home in their midst.   I noticed from
the very first that he was gradually beginning to put
aside the Italian cloak which he had worn for several weeks and was becoming a Frenchman again.
It was natural that he should do so.   But I also
noticed that in proportion as he was reclaimed to
his own nationality, I was passing out of Louis'
interests.   At last I found myself the only "for-

eigner" in the group. Presently, on the grounds
that I was an inefficient lumberman, I was dis-
charged.

I saw Louis just once after that. He was altogether a Frenchman again, but for one thing. Ever
since we had been together he had been wearing some
of my clothes, even though they were far too small
for him. Among other articles he had frequently
worn a pair of gray trousers, my Sunday-go-to-
meeting ones, in fact the only pair of to-day-I-am-
not-working pants I owned. Louis looked so funny
in them; they reached well above his ankles on his
thin mast-like legs and were tighter by far around
the hips than anything he must have worn in his
days before the mast. As I was about to leave the
camp, I demanded that he divest himself of my
precious belongings, but he refused. So I planned
my revenge. On the Sunday following my discharge,
I had settled down, as we will presently see, in Stacyville, and I felt a special need of my pantaloons. So
I decided I would go a-hunting for them. I borrowed a .38 rifle for the occasion, and strapping it
over my shoulder, soon after dinner I started on my
punitive errand. On reaching the camp, I squatted
myself under a tree, whose branches reached well
down to the ground and there I waited patiently for
the appearance of my trousers. They did not show
up all afternoon and at night I returned to Stacyville. The next Sabbath I started again on my hunt;

this time I took to the road with my rifle bright and early, thinking I might have a better chance to see my trousers walking about the camp. On reaching the spot I again hid myself under the trees, with the barrel of my gun pointing toward the door of the camp. All day long I lay there silent as a mouse. The pantaloons did not appear and it seemed as if they must have smelled a rat, for though everybody else came, I did not once see Louis. Finally, toward evening, I saw two men standing near the side of the camp. I could not see their faces, but on careful scrutiny, I observed the up-ankle appearance of my pants, and springing from my hiding-place I cocked my gun and suddenly faced Louis. "My pants or your life!" I seemed to say. Louis stood petrified before me. I ordered him to dismantle himself then and there, or I would shoot. He did not move. Just then two other men came out from the camp. Knowing the true condition of my gun, and fearing a sudden attack from all present, I began to retreat slowly. As they came toward me I turned heel and fled without firing a single shot, for I had made sure to leave every last cartridge at the house, not wishing to inflict any injury on my best trousers or on the thin legs within them.

So I returned to Stacyville pantless, panting and forlorn, and I never saw my trousers any more. When years afterward, I learned the song "Nellie Gray," visions of my pantaloons would loom before me as I sang, "I'll never see my trousers any more."

E GO TO JAIL

[There was a] breaking heart beneath the stars,
Tho' the hushed earth lay smiling in the light,
And the dull fetters and the prison bars
Saw bitter tears of agony that night,
And heard such burning words of love and truth
As wring the life-drops from the heart of youth.
                                        Phoebe Carey.

CHAPTER V

THE reader will understand that on the day I left Louis and the camp my feelings were far from joyous. Here I was, all alone, the only real companion I had in America forever gone. I was far away from Boston and farther than ever from my dream of returning home. By evening I reached the depot at Stacyville, and sitting down upon the station platform I put my face in my hands and began to meditate upon all that had transpired from the time I left home years before to the present. Whenever I think of that scene, there comes to my mind the picture of the Prodigal Son. But in that parable there was no ocean, no foreign country, and it was comparatively easy for the son to return to his father. If some of those difficulties had been considered in the story, I am sure it would hold a very deep significance for foreign boys in this country. I have no doubt that many of them at times are filled with deep yearnings to return to their fathers' houses, but the distance is too great, the ocean is too big, and they cannot go.

As I sat on the platform, I lived again in my memory all the years of my wanderings. An inexpressible longing seized me to return to my people across the sea. As I write these lines, in the rest hours of this Sunday morning, I wonder how many thousands of immigrant boys are finding life a lonely game in this country and are hungering for their loved ones at home.

I arose, gritting my teeth. Then walking up to the station master, I told my story, and offering him the seventy-five cents which I had, I asked him to sell me a ticket to the nearest place where I could find even one Italian. I longed just to talk to some one in my own tongue. But he shook his head; the nearest place was Millinocket, and seventy-five cents was not enough to take me there. Just then a man drove up with a load of potatoes. The station master explained my predicament to him and asked him if he did not want a young man to work for him. Right then and there George Annis, for that was his name, offered me work on his farm at $15 a month, with board, room and washing. It seemed very good to me. In two or three months I would earn enough for my return passage to Italy. So I helped him unload his potatoes and drove back with him to his farm, about two miles from the Stacyville depot.

Stacyville is one of those small hamlets so often found in the sparsely settled sections of our country,

consisting of a rickety depot, a few houses, un-
painted for a generation; a store in which you can
buy anything from a cobble nail to a feather for a
lady's hat; a weatherbeaten old building which dares
to assume the dignified name of "church," and where
a few old ladies and gentlemen look at everybody
over their glasses; these made up what is called a
"village." In Stacyville there was not even a church.
Evidently the residents of this "village" did not
believe in having religion intrude itself in their
affairs. Occasionally in the winter time, when there
was not much to do, a young minister from a neigh-
boring village held services, but that was all. It is
a prevalent idea that the city is the abode of wickedness and vice, while the country life is free from
temptations of this sort. This may be true in some
communities in which I have not been privileged to
live, but it certainly was not so of Stacyville. I
have never in all my life heard such obscene, filthy,
profane language as I heard used by the men of
that village. The oaths of the old Tuscan sailor
on board the *Francesco* were mild in comparison to
it. The women too, on occasion, were not averse to
the use of the same kind of choice phrases. Some
of the women smoked, not the delicate cigarette of
the New Yorker, but odoriferous old pipes. Liquor
flowed freely, though it was in prohibition Maine,
and there were one or two houses of ill repute. And
so I might go on describing the life of this first

village which I, a foreigner, was to come to know intimately. From these people I learned my first lessons in English and my first lessons in American life and manners.

I was much pleased at the outset to learn that George Annis was an *American*. Thus far I had come into personal contact with an Italian barber; Louis, a Frenchman; my "padrone," an Italian; the factory superintendent, a Swede; and my boss at the lumber camp, a Scandinavian. All the while I had wondered what an American employer was like. So I was pleased to have George Annis as my prospective "boss."

The first event of importance which occurred in my life in this American home was the changing of my name. George Annis, who I discovered later was almost illiterate, could not pronounce what he called my "Eyetalian" name. So he proposed to change it. I was at first bewildered and wondered what my relatives would think, since they had given me my name to perpetuate that of my grandfather. But I wanted to be as much as possible like an American, and there seemed to be no way out of it, so George changed my unpronounceable Italian name to one that was genuinely American.

This is not an uncommon experience among immigrants in this country. Some make a change on their own initiative, for the sake of convenience, or in order to be Americans at least in name. **By far**

the greater number of changes, however, are super-
imposed by employers. In either case, some of the
changes are truly humorous. Dr. Edward Steiner in
one of his books, tells the story of a young Italian
whose name was Giovanni Salvini. Having lived in
this country for a period,—it must have been in
Boston,—he decided to change his name. He began
to cast about to find some genuine American name
which he might adopt as his own. At last he hit
upon one which was from its common use, to his way
of thinking, truly American. So he called himself
"Mike Sullivan."

The name which George Annis gave me, however,
far excelled that for its true American origin; in its
very atmosphere it was American, and fairly smelled
of Americanism. For a period of some three months
I was known as "Mr. Beefsteak." When I discovered
its true significance, I naturally objected to passing
for Italian tenderloin. Then George gave me a
second name, Frank Nardi, which stayed with me
until I entered school and was able to assume my
own name again. Meanwhile, I was ashamed to ac-
knowledge to my people at home that I had consented to the change of my name, and I sent them
envelopes addressed to "Mr. Frank Nardi" and directed them to insert in these sealed letters bearing
my proper name. Later I learned that this is
precisely the practice resorted to by immigrants with
changed names.

At once I set myself to the task of learning English. My motive for this was twofold: First I realized that a knowledge of English was necessary to my work; and second, I wanted to acquire a knowledge of English so that on my return home in a few months I might become an interpreter like the old blind man I had seen in Molfetta years before. I applied myself to this task as best I could simply by listening to the speech of others, and in five months had gained a sufficient knowledge of English to provoke the remark that I was a "liar" when I said I had been in this country but a few months. Of course one thing was greatly to my advantage. This was the fact that there was not a single person in Stacyville who could speak Italian, so I was forced to use English at all times. In fact, it was fully three years before I spoke Italian again and then I found it difficult to say the first few words. It has been my observation that if young immigrants in the early stages of their life in this country have the opportunity to be separated from those who speak the native tongue, in a comparatively brief period they get a good grasp of the English language. And what is more, they come to understand the advantages of mingling with American people and to develop a wholesome attitude toward America and all things American.

But I started to tell the story of my first lessons in English. Soon after my arrival at the Annis farm, I was put at the task of picking up potatoes. We had two sets of barrels; I was instructed to put the large potatoes into one barrel and the small ones, together with those partly decayed, into another. In my eagerness to learn English, I asked John Brown, a fellow worker, "What call these?" pointing to the large potatoes. "Them are good, *good* potatoes," was his answer. As the most obvious quality was the *size*, rather than the goodness, of these potatoes, naturally "good" meant "large" to me. "And what them?" I inquired, pointing to the small and decayed potatoes. "Them are *rotten*," said Brown. In contrast with "large," "rotten" then meant "small" to me. The days passed and I felt quite happy in the thought of having learned two very essential words, "large" and "small." One day I saw a beautiful young colt going by. I called Gracie, the housekeeper's little girl, and asked her, "What call that?" "Colt," she said. Putting the two things together, I said, "That is a rotten colt." She laughed and I could not understand why. As no one enlightened me, I kept on using the two words "good" and "rotten" in the sense I understood them. Whenever I saw a small house, I would say: "That is a rotten house," or a small man, "That is a rotten man." And people laughed at my English!

George Annis also had some apples on the farm, and in the course of conversation often used the word "apples." Now any one acquainted with

Italian knows that the word Naples in its first syllable is pronounced very much like "apples"; and every time the word was uttered I thought they were talking about me. This was perhaps due to the fact that I had been brought up to have a feeling of aversion for Naples because of the life of that city, and I was afraid Annis had taken me for a Neopolitan.

I worked on George Annis' farm until late fall, and in the winter I went into the woods with him and worked as "cookie" or assistant cook, in a lumbering camp of his own. In the early spring we returned to the farm. The time had at last come when I was ready to return to Italy. I had worked for six months: at $15 per month that meant $90. I had received only five dollars in cash, and that would leave $85 coming to me, which would certainly be sufficient to buy me a third class passage and leave something with which to purchase a few gifts to take back with me. In the meantime I had been in correspondence with an Italian bank in Boston and had made arrangements for them to reserve for "Frank Nardi" a third class passage for the middle of April. About the first of the month I went to Mr. Annis and asked him to pay me. He said he would do so in a few days. The middle of the month was now approaching and the time for my departure was near, so again I went to him. It was then that the truth came out. He laughed me out of court and with a sneer upon his lips which I remember to this very day, he handed me a five-dollar bill and said that that was all he could pay me.

I cannot well describe the feeling which came over me. It was as if the very earth had crumbled away under my feet; I was bitterly angry; I hated the man and I hated America with all the strength of my young soul. And as I reflect upon the incident and the feelings which surged through my being on that day, I understand why "foreigners" are so often suspicious, and why they so often have cause to feel anything but admiration or love for America and things American.

I was determined to have justice, however, and so decided to go to Boston and ask the assistance of an Italian lawyer in an effort to collect the money I had earned. To decide to do this was one thing. To carry out my decision was an entirely different matter. I went to the depot and offered the agent the five-dollar bill which Annis had given me, for a ticket to Boston. He shook his head and informed me it would take much more than that to buy a ticket for Boston. I tried to borrow some money, but failed. One day I confided in a young friend of mine, who disliked Annis, and he suggested a way whereby I could get to Boston without difficulty. He said it was often customary for a young fellow like me to jump on the first train that came along and go wherever he willed. He even specified the coal tender as the best place to ride. Of course

I had had no experience of this character, but I was desperate and decided to follow his advice and get to Boston in the way he had suggested.

In those days there were only two trains a day through Stacyville. Late one afternoon, I waited for the train, and, following the directions of my friend, I took my place on the back of the coal tender and seated myself as comfortably as possible, ready for the long trip. I do not quite understand how the engineer or some one of the train crew failed to see me, for I, unconscious that I was doing anything wrong, made no effort whatever to conceal myself, and in fact, got on from the same side that the passengers boarded the train. The train started on its journey, and as evening came on I began to grow cold. It was rather a sharp frosty night. All my clothing was still at Norcross, and I was thinly clad and felt the cold. I curled up next to the door of the baggage car and tried to go to sleep. It must have been about ten o'clock when we came to a siding, where the train stopped to allow a northbound express to go by. The engineer came out to look over his engine. Thinking it would warm me up a little if I should walk around for a moment, I jumped off the train and went up to the engineer. He looked at me in amazement and asked me what I was doing there. In broken English I told him my story, how I had lost my money and was going to Boston and

secure the help of a lawyer. He made no comment, and I got on the train again. I do not remember seeing any one else than the engineer. The
express went by and the train started once more.
As it sped on its way, every now and then the whistle
would peal forth its horrible shrieks, intensified by
the quietness of the night; and with the pouring in
of fresh coal, the flames would shoot up, leaving
long tracks of light against the darkness of the
sky.

A few moments after the train had started, the
door of the baggage car behind me suddenly opened
and I felt a hand taking hold of my collar and
pulling me in. It was the train-master. Doubtless
the engineer had in some way managed to let him
know that I was on the train. He pulled me to the
center of the car and asked me to sit down upon a
box. The other members of the train crew surrounded me, looking as if they were ready at any
moment to spring upon me. The train-master asked
me my name and where I lived, noting the answers
in a little book. I told him the whole story as best
I could, and when I was through he told me to stay
there and I was thankful, for it had grown very cold
outside.

It must have been about an hour later when the
train came to a stop at a station, which I learned
afterward was somewhere in Vermont. I had fallen
asleep and the next thing I knew a great big man

stood over me, shaking me by the shoulder. I awoke and answered several questions which he asked me. I understood him to say, "You stay in this town to-night. Come with me and I'll put you up." I took this as a matter of counsel, although I noticed that he grinned. But as I was very tired and sleepy, I gave it no thought and decided to follow his advice, thinking I would go on the next day. I was really thankful for his offer of shelter and thought to myself that after all Americans *were* kind to traveling strangers, as we were in Italy.

The big man took hold of my hand and led me through the dark streets. As he did so, the same sense of security came over me which I had felt as a small boy when my father would take me by the hand and lead me in the dark. I walked along, now and then saying a word or two to break the silence. We came to a narrow alley, which seemed darker than ever. The big man pulled a key from his pocket and opened a door. He led me in, still holding me by the hand, and locked the door from within. Then he lighted a small kerosene lamp, and I looked around. I said to myself, "What a funny sort of house this man lives in; he must be a hermit." It was a square room, with walls of bare bricks. There was no picture on the walls and not a sign of human habitation. To the right were two tiny rooms, more like small alcoves; in each was a small bunk-like arrangement with straw spread upon it.

He pointed to one of these and said, "You can sleep there for now." Then he began to move toward the door, while I looked at him in amazement. As he approached the door, still with his back to it, he took out the key and unlocked it with his hand behind him, still facing me. I reached for the lamp, which was on a little shelf in the alcove, thinking to give him more light. As I reached for it, he slipped out with a quick movement and turned the key from the outside. Then I saw the bars in the windows. With this the awful realization came over me: I was in jail.

I do not like to recollect what happened during the next few moments, or of the awful anguish of that night. It hurts me even yet to think of it. There was a flood of tears and cries from a soul wrung in bitter agony. Here in the face of cruel injustice and seeking a means of securing justice, I had been hurled into prison. What would they do with me now? The vivid stories of Silvio Pellico's prison experiences, which I had read when a boy, came back to my mind. Upon the wall were some scribbles in Italian to the effect that he who by chance should enter that cell would never leave it alive. What would they really do to me? Would they burn me? Hang me? Shoot me? No one who has not gone through a similar experience can fully realize the feelings that surged through me, crushing my very soul. How could I, with my scanty knowledge of English, explain my innocence? All that long night I spent standing by the bars, looking out toward the free world and wondering what would become of me. The silence was oppressive; my heart-throbs were like muffled drum-beats. Now and then, the sharp realization of what had happened came over me, and I would cry out in sheer bewilderment. I called for "mother" as only a child can cry when utterly lost and in despair.

It seemed years before the first gleams of light began to appear in the sky. I had had not a moment of rest. Quite early in the morning the blacksmith across the street opened his shop. I must have disturbed him during the night, for no sooner had he opened the doors than he came up to the bars through which I was looking and still crying. I thought he was coming to show me sympathy, but he spat into my face, saying something which I did not understand, then turned back to his anvil. Later, innocent little urchins and sweet little girls came and threw stones at me. It was about nine o'clock when I saw the big man coming toward the jail. He said he had come to take me to court. I plead with him to let me go, but he held me tightly in his grip and led me through the streets, while a crowd of little children followed. I was in a cold perspiration and trembling with exhaustion when we reached the court.

The moment I stepped into the courtroom and looked into the kindly face of the judge a feeling

of hope came over me. I felt certain I was looking
into the face of a friend who would comprehend.
There are moments in life when the spoken word is
not necessary to give us a glimpse of a soul. Instinctively I knew that I was standing before a man
who would deal justly and kindly with me. In
answer to the judge's questions, I precipitately told
my story. I offered him such letters as I had with
me, from my relatives and from the bank in Boston,
as a means of identification. I saw a light of understanding come over the kindly countenance of the
judge. He understood my predicament and ordered
me dismissed. He instructed the big man to brush
me off, give me a breakfast, take me to the depot and
buy me a ticket for Stacyville, the place from which
I had come. I presume this was in compliance with
the vagrancy law of the state. I asked no question and offered no objection. I was thankful to be
a free man again, even though I was being sent back
to Stacyville.

I can never be thankful enough to that kindly
old judge. I have often wished I might be able to
express to him my gratitude for his treatment of
me. He might well have condemned me to a re-
formatory or prison or heavily fined me, but he was
one of those really human judges, who in dealing with
a "foreigner" as well as a native, tempers the techni-
cality of the law with the warmth of human consideration. This often saves a youth from be-

coming a criminal. I presume, however, that somewhere in the police records of the state of Vermont, my name, alias "Frank Nardi," is to be found; along with thousands of other unfortunates, some of them doubtless as innocent as I. Doubtless also, somewhere a careful student of the criminal tendencies of the foreign-born people of this country has counted my name along with thousands of others in his impersonal statistical study of the criminality of the immigrant groups in the United States.

I AM CAUGHT AGAIN

I've seen a dove, storm-beaten, far at sea;
　　And once a flower growing stark alone
　　From out a rock; I've heard a hound make moan,
Left masterless: but never came to me
　　Ere this such sense of creatures torn apart
From all that fondles life and feeds the heart.
Richard Burton.

CHAPTER VI

O N reaching Stacyville where else could **I go** but back to Annis' farm? Of course **I** did not tell him all that had happened; but he realized that **I** had failed to carry out my threat of seeing a lawyer, and so made no end of ridiculing me. Soon after my return George Annis disappeared, and to this day **I** have no way of telling what became of him. It was hinted at the time that he had become so deeply involved in financial and moral difficulties that he had left for the West. **I** never heard more of him.

The farm now passed into the hands of Mr. John Carter. For a year or more Mrs. Carter had acted as general housekeeper and manager for Annis, and as he had not met his payments to her, he made a deal whereby Mr. and Mrs. Carter were to keep the farm for a certain period. It was now time for the annual planting of crops and John Carter asked me to remain with him, promising to pay me bi-weekly. As my hopes for an immediate return to Italy had vanished, **I** decided to work for him.

John Carter was a French-Canadian, of whom there are many in all parts of Maine. He was a short, stubby fellow with black mustache; quick in decision and action; and though comparatively speaking, an uneducated man, he was very shrewd and had a keen business sense. His one overruling passion, as will be presently seen, was to make money, not only from the farm but also from a nefarious traffic, in which I was to find myself deeply involved.

About three miles from the farm was a logging camp employing about five hundred men. Shrewd John Carter realized that where lumbermen were, liquor would somehow find its way, and from the sale of liquor some one would reap large profits. Moreover, he saw no reason why he should not be the one to derive this benefit.

The reader will recall that Maine was a prohibition state long before the Nineteenth Amendment was passed. Although it was not impossible to get liquor in the larger cities, such as Bangor, Augusta, Waterville and Portland, it was rather difficult to do so in the country districts and elude the authorities, especially if the sheriff was at all diligent in the performance of his duties, as was the case in the county in which Stacyville was located. John Carter knew all this and took every possible precaution against getting caught. One day he suggested that, as his handwriting was very poor, he would like to have me transcribe some letters which he had written. I made no objection and copied his letters, even signing his name on his instruction. As time went on, he asked me to do other things, such as sending in orders to a wholesale liquor firm in Boston, and sending all Money Orders. The liquors were being shipped to my name in his care.

He took the additional precaution of hiding the liquors very carefully. At first he concealed them in an unfurnished attic, access to which was had through a secret trap door which Carter built for the purpose. Later he hid them in the barn, under the floor, buried in the earth. Still later he took me with him to the woods bordering the farm, where we concealed the bottles in a hole which he had dug.

Now all this secrecy puzzled me considerably, so one day I asked Carter the reason for it. He said he was afraid the lumbermen might come in large numbers and, overwhelming us, seize the liquors. For the same reason I must be ready at a moment's notice to hide myself so they could not find me and force me to tell them where the liquors were hidden. One night he actually warned me to go to the woods and hide, for he feared they were coming. I climbed a tree and remained there all night long.

Of course looking back upon it, I can see through his whole scheme. But even then I cannot quite understand how human nature can descend to such depths as to take such a beastly advantage of an innocent youth. I was at this time about twenty years of age, inexperienced and entirely unsuspecting, ignorant of the laws of the state regarding the sale of intoxicants, or of the sentiment of the better classes of people regarding their use. So I went on, unwittingly conducting the nefarious traffic under the supervision of Carter, acting as a tool in his greedy and lawless hands.

One thing, however, troubled me considerably. In Italy, and in any country for that matter, liquors are sold by the lowest class of people, although they are consumed by the public in general. It wounded my pride deeply to realize that I was being compelled, in so short a time after coming to America, to descend so low in the social scale as to be selling liquors. I often wondered what my people would think of me if they knew what I was doing. There was one consoling thought, and that was that it need not last long. Carter was paying me $15 per month (he could well afford to do so), and in a little while I would be in a position to return home. My relatives and friends need never know anything about it. They actually do not know to this day.

This infamous game continued for about three months, and then the unexpected happened, and I was brought to realize the full significance of it. About the middle of August a country fair was held in Millinocket. Carter had laid in a good supply of liquors, and one evening, loading a double wagon, he started for the fair, taking me with him. On nearing the town, a mile or so from the place where the fair was being held, he drove into a patch of woods and unloaded the liquors. Then he proceeded, with my help, to bury them. He gave the same reason for this as for hiding the liquor at the farm. He instructed me to take out one bottle at a time, and when I saw some one coming, give him the bottle upon his producing a dollar and a quarter; then take out the next bottle, and so on. I wanted to go and see the fair, but he would not let me, saying he had to go himself and drum up trade.

I sat in the woods waiting for the trade to come, and soon it did come. In the course of three or four hours I had sold about a dozen bottles. Toward evening I saw a man coming toward me through the woods at mad speed. I took him to be a thief, and made ready for an encounter. It was a young man whom I had never seen before. As he came up to me, he said, "Run, Frank, run!" I thought to myself, "Go on, young man, you cannot fool me," and remained unmoved. When he saw I would not stir he shouted: "For God's sake, man, run. The sheriff is coming." "Sheriff?" said I in bewilderment. Then like a flash I recalled my prison experience. But why should they take me now? I was at a loss to understand, but impressed with the earnestness of the young messenger, I took myself deeper into the woods. Suspecting foul play, I did not go very far, but lying low on the ground, I watched to see what was going on. The sheriff did come, I recognized him from his badge, but he did not find me nor the liquor. It was then the realization came over me that Carter had played me false. For a moment I thought I would come out boldly and tell the sheriff the whole story. But the thought of my previous jail experience and my fear of Carter held me back.

As the full truth dawned upon my mind, I was seized with a deeper feeling of despair than ever before. Again I saw my dream of home fading away into oblivion. I went from spot to spot aimlessly, wringing my hands and tearing my hair, wondering what would become of me next. Finally I reached the summit of a knoll, and throwing myself flat upon the ground, I buried my face in the earth. What to do next? How to find Carter? How to get back to Stacyville? How to get home? . . . These and a thousand other questions passed through my bewildered mind.

The sun was now sinking below the western horizon; the birds were chirping their good-night songs; the sweet odors of the forest were wafted on the cool evening breezes; the leaves were rustling gently. Nature was at peace, silent. But in my soul there was tumult, anger, despair, longing. My heart was throbbing violently. Moments seemed like years. "As there are years in which man does

not live a moment, so there are moments in which
one lives a lifetime." In those moments I lived years.
I was lying thus on the ground when the silence was
broken by the sound of approaching hoofs. I
realized I was not far from the road. "Can it be
Carter returning to Stacyville, without even trying
to find me?" I thought. In any case, how was I
to discover in the semi-darkness whether it was he,
without exposing myself. For might it not be the
sheriff hunting for me? Just then the team came
to a full stop opposite the place where I was hiding.
One of the horses neighed. It was Dick, my Dick,
the horse that I loved best, and used to feed sugar
and apples to. There are times when it seems that
the fidelity of a dumb animal exceeds by far the
loyalty of human beings. At least it seems free
from selfishness. In his instinctive way, Dick had
felt my presence near, and I knew his voice.

In a subdued tone some one called, "Frank . . .
Frank . . ." It was Carter's voice. I rose and
walked out to the road. I felt a bitter, almost
murderous anger toward the man. It is at such
moments that the inheritance of one's early training
comes into play with unseen power, either to save
him from possible ruin or to plunge him into some
disastrous act. And I am profoundly thankful for
the restraining power and the sense of honor which
I had inherited, which withheld my hand. Otherwise, I dare not think what I might have done as I

approached the wagon and Carter. I poured forth
upon him all the vials of righteous wrath; I called
him a coward and a fool, a traitor to God and man.
Soon calming down, however, I climbed into the
wagon beside him, and we started on. Carter had
recovered the liquor which was hidden in the woods,
and which in my flight I had abandoned.

We moved on in the deepening darkness. I spoke
not a word. The heavens were clear and dotted with
innumerable stars, whose gleam cast a pale light
upon our way. Presently, thick clouds began to
roll up before us; a thunderstorm was approaching.
Lightning flashes cleaved the sky, blinding us and
frightening the horses. Raindrops began to fall. A
sudden fear seized me. Could it be that John Carter,
fearing that I might carry out my threat to report
him to the authorities, would slay me on this desolate
road, under cover of the storm, and leave my body
by the roadside? I knew that he always carried a revolver. An awful shiver passed through me. What
suggested that thought I cannot say; thoughts
are said to pass from mind to mind in unexpected
ways.

Just then we approached a house. Seizing the
opportunity, I suggested that as it was raining so
hard, we should ask shelter for the night. He as-
sented, and I went up and knocked at the door. It
seemed as though the house was abandoned; for
twenty minutes or more we knocked and knocked,

but no one answered. At last a voice was heard from within. We asked for shelter, and after much argument, the man opened the door. He had a gun in his hand. He finally consented to house us for the night, and caring for our horses, we went to bed. By that time I had regained my spirits, and that night Carter and I slept, or attempted to sleep, in a bed actually covered with vermin, such as I had never seen before or have seen since in all my wanderings. The next morning we drove to Stacy-ville.

Life was now becoming hopeless in the extreme. I began to suspect every one with whom I came in contact and to doubt whether there was such a thing as right or justice. Here I had worked for nearly a year in an attempt to earn sixty or seventy dollars to return home, and I had been deceived at every turn, and those whom I trusted had proved to be traitors. I had made sacrifices; I had been sub-jected to humiliation, to reach a worthy goal, only to be taken advantage of, only to find myself penn-less, and what was infinitely worse, to be forced into a life of lawlessness. Those who would understand the so-called waves of crime and lawlessness among the non-English speaking groups in this country, need to know something of experiences such as these. Then and then only will they comprehend why help-less human beings, facing injustice and treachery, become reckless; while society hurls them into dungeons as outcasts or criminals. Now that it is all over, I am thankful for these experiences, for they have taught me to know and understand the struggles of humanity, especially of the "foreigner" in this country.

As it is in the life of a nation, so it is in the life of an individual. At every critical moment, some one rises up to guide and direct. In the life of a nation it is the statesman who rises to the emergency; in the life of an individual it is often some humble soul who furnishes the needed help and guidance. Often it is a woman!

A MYSTERIOUS EVENT

For a bitter night and day they shall be tried,
They shall moan within the cruel hands of greed;
But ever when the wrong has wrought its worst
Shall rise Redeemers answering to their need.
From some backwood Bethlehem
Their Christ shall come to them;
Through the roaring hells of Mammon, by the path
Of mocking Calvaries, he shall pass on in his wrath
Till his hands have hewn the way
To the daylight and the day.

William James Dawson.

CHAPTER VII

I n my case it was Mrs. Carter's mother. The dear old lady happened to be visiting her daughter at this time. I told her something of my early life and of the bitter struggle I had been making for months in an effort to make my way back home. She listened patiently. One day she frankly admitted that John Carter was a bad man; she would advise me to leave him at once. She offered to find me another place to work if I wished, on the one condition that I should tell no one that she had been responsible for my leaving, as Carter might do her harm. She said she had a son in Sherman, six miles away, and she would try to get me a job with or through him. I took her friendly advice and awaited developments.

It was while waiting for an answer from Sherman that an event, strange from the purely human point of view, occurred. As it helped to change the whole course of my life, I will simply relate it here and will leave it to the reader to draw his own conclusions. In the little brick schoolhouse in the village of

Stacyville, a zealous young Baptist preacher was holding evangelistic services. One evening John Brown, in one of his drunken fits, asked me to "go to church" with him. We have already seen that my religious teaching had been very scanty, and my ideas about Protestantism were not at all favorable, as I had been taught that this was atheism and the worship of Satan. Knowing that these were Protestant services, I refused to be contaminated by attending. I did not go that night, nor the following, but Brown kept insisting; so on the third evening I went, thinking perhaps it would do me no harm.

Three of us went together. We seated ourselves in the back seats, which, later I learned, evangelist preachers call "sinners' seats." I listened to the songs and the preaching, though I could not understand what the preacher was saying, nor the meaning of the songs. But during the meeting something strange gripped the very soul of me. What really happened I cannot tell, but something very real and powerful was transpiring in my consciousness. Although neither that experience or any subsequent one made me very religious, in the strictly Puritan sense of the word, yet for the first time I thought of life in terms of service. What relation the experiences of the preceding months had to the condition which made me susceptible to the influence of this atmosphere I cannot say. It is exceedingly difficult from the human point of view to explain such occurrences.

A week or so after this an answer came from Sherman and I left Stacyville to see it no more. Thus came to an end one of the strangest and most trying periods of my early life in America. George Annis, whom I had thought a real American, had turned out to be one of the most unscrupulous persons I have ever known. His gods were gluttonous eating, drinking, carousing, gambling, and indulging in all kinds of questionable practices. John Carter was not much better. Stacyville I had found to be a hotbed of all forms of iniquity. There where I was to get my first glimpses of what I thought was a representative American community, I had heard the vilest and most profane language. Men and women alike indulged in all kinds of questionable speech. Words possessing perfectly wholesome connotation were given the filthiest of meaning, and thus a part of the English language was forever soiled for me. Unprofessional prostitution was not uncommon. Liquor was sold in open defiance of the law. Threats of murder were frequently heard; lawlessness in game hunting was the boast of all; cattle stealing was not unknown, and there in that little hamlet of not over five hundred souls were to be found some of the lowest microbes of our national life. In that community I had been subjected to the most humiliating insults and torments. I had been the prey of the cheapest and lowest dregs of human society. Had I succeeded in getting back to Italy at this stage I certainly should have carried with me an ugly picture of America and things American. And I do not hesitate to assert that thousands upon thousands of "foreigners" have only that kind of a picture of America to look upon throughout their lives.

FIRST GLIMPSES

OF THE REAL AMERICA

A little cottage, and a garden-nook,
  With outlooks brief and sweet
Across the meadows, and along the brook,—
  A little stream that nothing knows
Of the great sea to which it gladly flows,—

  .   .   .   .

Here friendship lights the fire, and every heart,
Sure of itself and sure of all the rest,
Dares to be true, and gladly takes its part
In open converse, bringing forth its best:
And here is music, melting every chain
  Of lassitude and pain:
And here, at last, is sleep with silent gifts.

Henry Van Dyke.

CHAPTER VIII

KIND Mrs. Boynton (Mrs. Carter's mother) made arrangements whereby I was to go to her son's home in Sherman until I could find work. Accordingly, walking to the little village, I entered a new environment, in which I was to get the first glimpses of the real American.

Another hard experience, however, awaited me there. Mr. Boynton was a lumberman; he was also a heavy drinker and a gambler. He was a large man with hard, pronounced features, brusque in manner and a veritable brute in the treatment of his wife, who was a little woman, and looked so helpless by his side. She was a French-Canadian by birth and possessed all the versatility and warmth of the French, together with the common sense of the American. Her husband was so shiftless that she had a difficult task in endeavoring to keep body and soul together for herself and her two little children. But she was as plucky as she was enduring in the face of the hard lot which was hers.

I had been in this home two or three days when Mr. Boynton asked me to lend him some money. How he found out that I had a little money I do not know. I had managed by this time to accumulate about $50. I had grown so suspicious of everybody that I hesitated to lend even one cent. Mr. Boynton told me, however, that I could not remain in his home unless I loaned him $10. Mrs. Boynton, perhaps fearing that her husband would spend the money on drinks and give her the usual beating which followed one of his drinking bouts, called me aside and counselled me not to give him a cent. She further advised me to go to Houlton and deposit all I had in a bank. The next morning I disappeared, and going to Houlton, I made my first deposit of $40 in an American bank.

On my return the next day I witnessed a very pathetic scene. Either Mrs. Boynton had told her husband what she had advised me to do or he suspected it. He threatened to kill her with an ax. The plucky little woman drew a revolver and for a moment I thought I would witness a murder. Fortunately, however, nothing serious happened.

I now started out by myself to find work, and this time fortune really favored me. I went to the house of a farmer, Mr. Frank Richmond, who gave me a job, and so at last I found myself in a genuine American home.

Mr. Richmond was a typical, native-born New England "Yankee." He was a man of genuine goodness and dignity. He wore a goatee and a straw hat similar to what we see in pictures representing Uncle Sam. Often when I see a cartoon of Uncle Sam I think of Mr. Richmond. His Sunday-go-to-meeting clothes were also of the type worn by our national relative. Moreover, he possessed a keen sense of humor, and had that enduring patience on the one hand and that vehement tenacity of purpose on the other which we often associate with our good National Uncle.

Mr. Richmond was usually patient with me, inexperienced as I was in farming and doing farm chores, but I soon discovered another side to his nature. One day he put me to work splitting wood in the wood-shed, which was located next to the kitchen. Desiring to look at one of his beautiful daughters who was at work in the kitchen, I left the wood block and taking my ax, I began to split wood on the doorstep, near the kitchen door. In doing so I made a few dents in the steps. Mr. Richmond happened to come in, and seeing what I had done, he began to pour forth a volley of the choicest epithets imaginable, most of which are not to be found in the dictionary. But I had a staunch defender, Mr. Richmond's eldest daughter. Doubtless she herself had been subjected to such onslaughts and therefore knew where to throw in the first lines of defense. She came to my rescue and a lively scene ensued, which diverted the rapid fire from defenseless me.

Mrs. Richmond was the most beautiful character in the home, and possessed a deep spiritual loveliness. She had a dignity, a refinement, an ease of manner, a kindly and gentle spirit which made her truly "the first lady of the land" to me. Hers was not a house in which people merely live, but a true home, a true American home, as I have come to know it, in which are blended order and cleanliness, courtesy and frankness, consideration and ease, simplicity and sturdy morality. From the first day I entered her home Mrs. Richmond made me feel as one of her family, and thus a new day dawned in the history of my life in America.

There were five daughters in the home, all of whom were most considerate and courteous in their treatment of me. They were refined and possessed that genuine loveliness and reserve which makes a young woman of good breeding so inexpressibly attractive. Two of them were older than myself, two about the same age as I, and one, sweet little Beatrice, was about seven years old and a veritable little angel. Her sweetness bound a cord around my heart which still holds to this day. In the months which followed, my life with these people was so pleasant that the feeling of abhorrence I had come to have for American life was entirely counteracted, and I had my first taste of the real America I came to love. What would have been impossible in an Italian household often took place in this home. I associated freely with the young women, and often one of them was left alone with me. I was not sure which one was queen of my secret affections.

Both Mr. and Mrs. Richmond were devout and practical Christian people; in their home life was practised the simple religious customs of saying prayer at meals, and of family Bible reading and prayer. Their religion was a matter of everyday use and this impressed me profoundly. On Sunday afternoons the entire family would gather around the organ and have a religious "sing." If seems as if I can still hear that family singing, Mr. Richmond with his rich bass voice enjoying it immensely.

On Sundays they also attended church service and Sunday School regularly. Naturally they took me with them, and though I was a so-called Catholic I had no objection to going to any place where these splendid people went. Some of my first experiences in connection with attending these meetings are worth mentioning. I remember very well my first day in Sunday School. A Mr. Butterfield was teaching the young men's class. The lesson was in the Old Testament and had to do with David. The first question which he asked was directed to me: "Who was David?" As I had never seen a Bible in my life before entering the Richmond household and did not even know what a Sunday School quarterly was, the question naturally embarrassed me greatly and I was completely dumfounded. I could have told him very much better the way to the Inferno— Dante's, of course—but politeness interfered.

The middle-aged preacher, who came from Patten to preach in our country-side schoolhouse, I liked very much. He took a kindly interest in me from the very first. His pulpit teachings, however, seemed very strange to me. From his preaching and from what I gathered from other sources it seemed that it was sinful to bathe, to shave, to manicure, or even to laugh on Sunday. To take a walk or go for a ride was equally wicked, also to whistle or sing any but a religious tune. To read other than a religious book was not a good thing. A novel was always to be condemned. To attend a gay concert, an entertainment or the theater was very wicked. Now all this seemed very peculiar, but desiring to be like these Puritans while with them, I tried my best to do as they did, and believe as they believed, although I must admit that it was *very hard work*.

My second Christmas in America I spent with the Richmonds. They had the usual festivities and it was in that home I saw the first Christmas tree. I had learned of the custom of giving presents to others, so stealing away to Patten one night, I spent five dollars, all the ready money I had, to buy a present for every member of the household. I did not hang the presents on the tree but hid them where each could find his own, as we used to do with the Christmas letters we wrote to father and mother at home. On the tree there was a little present for me, however. It was a small copy of the New Testament. I was much pleased with it and immediately set myself to the task of reading it, not so much because it was the New Testament as because it was a book in English. That Testament became my reading book in the months that followed. I soon discovered that there was much more than English in it. The book of Romans made a special appeal to me, chiefly because it made me feel proud to have been a descendant of the people to whom the writer had addressed the letter. The twelfth chapter, however, went much deeper. It was the first piece of moral and religious teaching which I understood. That passage so perfect in diction, so lofty in sentiment, so genuinely practical in its teaching, appealed to me profoundly. I set out to memorize it and soon did so. Often I sat up late into the night, shivering in my cold attic room, reading and memorizing that chapter. It was the first passage of any nature that I learned to repeat in the English language, and I have never memorized anything better since.

This memory work made me eager to learn more, and it was at this point that the oldest daughter in the Richmond household came to play a decisive part in my life. She was the teacher of the grade school at the little country schoolhouse. She came to have a deep interest in me, and I in her. She it was who was to cause *the great awakening* in my life. What story like this is devoid of some romance? She never lost an opportunity to hint at the great subject and I to take inspiration from it. I hesitated a long time, not knowing what consequences such a step might lead to. I feared that it might divert me from my purpose to return home. Finally I plucked up courage. It was late on a moonlight evening. I was still in doubt, but at last, hesitatingly as a boy will, I offered myself to her and she accepted me and I became her . . . pupil. It was no love match, nothing of the kind, but only an awakening to return to school and to books.

"MY BOY,
YOU OUGHT TO
GO TO SCHOOL"

Know you the meaning of all they are doing?
Know you the light that their soul is pursuing?
Know you the might of the world they are making,
This nation of nations whose heart is awaking?
What is this mingling of peoples and races?
Look at the wonder and joy in their faces!

Alfred Noyes.

CHAPTER IX

"MY BOY, YOU OUGHT TO GO TO SCHOOL"

THE next day I entered Miss Richmond's school. It was about six years since I had left school in Italy. Now I returned to it of my own volition. But soon both Miss Richmond and I discovered that there were other factors to be considered than my willingness to go to school and her desire to teach me. The school, of course, was held in the usual one-roomed schoolhouse so common in the country districts. What happened on the first and second days the reader can easily imagine. Here was a young man twenty years of age sitting in the midst of children ranging from six to fourteen. Not only this, but he knew very little English and had been away from school so long he hardly knew how to handle a book. The test was too great for human nature. The children immediately began to poke fun at the new pupil, to call him names, to throw paper wads at him and torment him in every way, until neither Miss Richmond nor I had a moment of peace the whole day long. It was clear from the very first that it was an impossible situation. I stood it for about a week, then Miss Richmond suggested that I take private lessons at home, to which I gladly consented.

It was then that I set out to learn English in real earnest. Miss Richmond sent to New York for a Webster Abridged Dictionary and giving me a copy of Ainslee's Magazine, she started me on my way to master the language. I have always been thankful that Miss Richmond started me out in this way. She could not have known anything about the so-called "translation method" of teaching English to foreigners. If she did, she must have realized that I would learn more in one day by directly mastering English words, phrases and idioms than I would in a year by the thumb-hunting way of translation. I have discovered that the translation method leads a pupil to give seventy-five per cent of his attention to his native tongue and the remainder to English. What he needs is exactly the reverse. In the way Miss Richmond taught me English I found I was not only acquiring the language rapidly, but I was also learning the roots of words and through that means was getting at the soul of the language.

My motive now was fundamentally different than at first, as I faithfully applied myself to learning the language. At first I had desired to learn English primarily that I might, on my return to Italy, become an interpreter; also that I might better be able to earn enough money to take me back to Italy. Now my desire to learn the language was based upon my interest in the family with whom I was living. I wanted to be able to understand these people who had been so kind and considerate to me, and I wanted to be able to convey to them my ideas and my feelings.

Late that winter I left the Richmonds intending to return to them, but events so shaped themselves that I did not go back again to that beautiful home. In the vicinity of Skowhegan, Maine, lived the Butterfield brothers, relatives of the Richmonds. They were lumbering on their own account, and being in need of help and knowing that Mr. Richmond had no need of my services during the winter months, they requested that I be sent down to them. I hesitated about going, but as I was told that I was coming back, I went.

I had been with the Butterfields about a week when one day, it was the 10th of March, 1904, Mr. William Butterfield and I were sawing a log which we had felled the night before. I was pulling one end of the cross-cut saw, he the other, when all of a sudden, Mr. Butterfield stopped and looked at me intently. As he did so the village clock in the distance was ringing seven strokes, which echoed through the frosty air of that March morning. As if struck by a new thought, Mr. Butterfield, with emphasis, said to me: "Frank, my boy, you ought to go to school." That and no more. I made no answer and we went on with our work. But his words kept echoing through my consciousness as a sort of challenge. How could I go to school? I was going back to Italy! Then I had no money and no friends to help me out.

One Sunday afternoon a week or so after this incident, I went up to my room and throwing myself upon my bed I fell asleep. On awakening, I saw a copy of the Lewiston Journal lying on a chair alongside the bed and reaching for it, I began to turn the pages casually. My eyes soon became riveted upon one page. On it was printed the story of an Italian lad, who starting as an illiterate, had entered school, had graduated, gone to a theological seminary and had become a successful pastor. It seemed like a bugle call sounding a note of inspiration. I remembered Mr. Butterfield's words. I arose, went to the closet, packed up my few belongings and with calm resolution determined to go to school at once. How I was to get there, how I was to pay my way, I did not know; I only felt an absolute certainty that somehow I would go to the school where the poor Italian lad of the story had gone.

It was no small task which I had unconsciously set before me. I went downstairs and told the Butterfield brothers of my decision. Much to my surprise, they began to ridicule the idea. To think of my starting off to school without money! It was true I had only about fifty dollars, all I had saved in the year and a half I had been in this country, but I reasoned, "Did not this Italian boy go to school without even a cent of money?" When I reminded Mr. Butterfield of the words he had spoken to me only two weeks before, he answered, "Sure, I told you to go to school, Frank, but you must save some money first." His reasoning was in vain; nothing could turn my mind from my resolve. I would enter school at any cost, and *now*.

In the face of the discouraging attitude the Butterfields had taken toward the proposition, I now decided to go to the village and endeavor to enlist the help of the pastor of one of the churches. I attended the prayer meeting that very evening, and at the close I asked the pastor if I might not have his counsel on a matter. He took me to the parsonage and I told him of my desire to attend school. I asked him if he would not be so good as to write the president of the school a letter asking him to give me an opportunity to work my way. He said, "I am sorry I can't do that; I don't know you and I don't see how I can recommend you." He gave me the name and address of the president, however, and suggested that I write him myself, and with that he dismissed me. I was frozen to the core by his stiff attitude and as I went out into the night my hopes began to flicker.

My original determination was soon renewed, however, and I decided to take another tack. I would write to the Italian pastor whose story had awakened my interest to enter school; he would certainly help me. So I wrote him a letter,—a mixture of Italian and English,—and for a week I waited impatiently for his answer. Daily I would go to the post-office, and receiving no mail in the morning, I would loiter about the streets or in the public library while waiting for other mails to arrive. Often I would wait for hours at the same spot, on the corner near the post-office.

I must have aroused the interest, if not the suspicions, of a policeman, for one morning he came up to me and began to ask me all kinds of questions: who I was, where I lived, what was my nationality, my trade, and what was I doing on that street corner so often. I answered his questions and told him that I was waiting for a letter from a friend. He told me to "move along" and I did. Finally one day the long-expected letter came. It was a very formal, typewritten note, in English; it gave the name and address of the school and advised me to write to the president telling him of my desires, though he did not give me the name of the president. The last part of the note was devoted to a piece of advice. In my letter to him I had written "I am *sorrow* to trouble you," and his advice was that I should write "I am *sorry* to trouble you." That was the most specific part of the letter. Again I felt somewhat bewildered and once more I found myself loitering on the street corner, this time staring into the air.

Just then the policeman came along and I told him I had received the letter. I must have shown my disappointment and anxiety. He asked me to go with him; my previous prison experience, however, made me suspicious, and I hesitated, but finally followed him, not knowing where he would lead me to, and for that reason keeping at arm's length. I feared he might play a trick on me as the other policeman had done. We went on, and for a few moments I thought my fears were going to be realized, for he was heading for police headquarters. Could it be that one could be put into jail for wanting to go to school?

MY AMERICAN EDUCATION

AND ITS MEANING

What constitutes a school?
Not ancient halls and ivy-mantled towers,
  Where dull traditions rule
With heavy hand youth's lightly springing powers;
  Not spacious pleasure courts,
And lofty temples of athletic fame,
  Where devotees of sports
Mistake a pastime for life's highest aim;
  Not fashion, nor renown
Of wealthy patronage and rich estate;
  No, none of these can crown
A school with light and make it truly great.
  But masters, strong and wise,
Who teach because they love the teacher's task,
  And find their richest prize
In eyes that open and in minds that ask.
   .   .   .   .
  Ah, well for him who gains
In such a school apprenticeship to life:
  With him the joy of youth remains
In later lessons and in larger strife!
                    Henry Van Dyke.

CHAPTER X

I WAS about to turn on my heels and run for the country and the Butterfields' when he beckoned gently. I stepped in, still seriously in doubt as to the possible outcome. Once inside the police station, I realized that he meant to transact other business than placing me in jail. He sat down on one side of a big table and I on the other. He asked me what I wanted to write to the president of the school. I told him: I was a poor boy; I had no money; I wanted to go to school; I had read about the poor Italian boy who had gone to this school, and wanted a chance to work my way. The police-man wrote it down. The letter was brief and to the point. He read it over to me, his face beaming with a smile of satisfaction. Then he asked me to copy it in my own hand. I did so, and we mailed the letter. Then the policeman took me to a good boarding-house where I stayed while waiting for an answer. Each day I went to the post-office and met my policeman friend on the corner or at the police station to report results. A week passed and no answer. One morning he said, "Something's gone wrong, my boy. You'd better go on. The president sure'll give you a chance."

That same afternoon, with a suitcase of belongings and an old brown overcoat over my arm, I was off for school. Officer Allen, for that was the policeman's name, took me to the depot, loaned me his mileage; gave me an addressed envelope for its return; put me on the right train; told the conductor my story and asked him to be sure to put me off at Readfield. He stood and waved "good-by" as the train pulled out of the station. What a friend that policeman was to me! What a friend every policeman could be to the "foreigner" and what a service he could render to our country!

What had become of my letter to the president and why had I received no answer? It will be recalled that the Skowhegan minister had declined to write a letter for me and that he had given me the name and address of the president verbally. When officer Allen addressed the envelope for me I dictated "Mr. W. F. Merry," as I had understood the minister to say, instead of Mr. W. F. Berry, Kent's Hill, Maine. Accordingly, the letter was not delivered. Six months later, desiring to discover what had become of it, I made inquiries and found it buried in the post-office.

It may be of interest to state that the minister

who had refused to help me later, upon learning of my success in school and noting that my name was receiving some slight mention in the press, claimed the credit of having directed me to the school. His wife even published an article regarding the matter.

At about noon, on April 17, 1904, I stepped off the train at Readfield, four miles from the Maine Wesleyan Seminary, my objective. I was told there was a stage which went "up the hill" and that it would cost only fifty cents to ride. As I had exactly seventy-five cents in my pocket and did not know what awaited me at the end of my journey, I decided to walk. Taking my suitcase in one hand and my overcoat in the other I started on my upward road. As I passed by the stage I heard a man say, "Fools ain't all dead yet," but did not realize then that it was directed at me. I had gone a short distance from the depot when I saw a wagon coming out from a house, headed toward the hill. To make certain that I was going in the right direction I made inquiries of the driver. He said he too was going to "the hill" and would be glad to have me ride with him. I climbed in alongside of him. At once I felt a sense of security and that I had found a friend. He asked me about myself and I told him my story. He was at once interested and offered words of encouragement and helpfulness. Weeks afterward I learned that he was the son of the late Dr. Chase, former president of the school. He gave

me much information and advice and even took me
to the office of the president and introduced me to
Professor H. E. Trefetheren, subsequently professor
of Greek at Colby College, and at that time acting
president of the school.

From the moment I set foot on the "Hill" I felt
an atmosphere of friendliness and helpfulness.
Professor Trefetheren at once endeavored to find
work and shelter for me. By night I had my
first job. The work was to saw three cords of
wood which was so dry that every boy who had
tried it had given up in disgust. I received $3.50
per cord for sawing and splitting. It took me about
two weeks. I was told years afterward that a woman
who saw me at this task remarked that in that boy
was good timber for an American. I hope this was
true, but I certainly would not wish to be sawing
that kind of timber all my life.

The day following my arrival I was hard at work
on my studies in the preparatory class. I was very
happy in my new environment. But a few days later
my troubles began to brew. Late one afternoon,
much to my astonishment, a young lady student
came to me after class and very pleasantly invited
me to take a walk with her. It was very sudden, and
it embarrassed me greatly. But thinking it the
custom in this country for a young lady to make
such advances, I made no objection but meekly
followed her lead "armed and well prepared." We

walked toward the lower part of the campus. We came to a large tree and sat down under it. The matter was growing serious! She started the conversation by saying something about my knife. Now I have already related how I had lost my beautiful knife on my first excursion into the woods, a knife which had come down to me as a heirloom. It seemed very mysterious to me that she should know anything about my knife, but thinking that perhaps in some strange way she had come into possession of it, I began describing it to her: a black-handled knife with two blades and a silver seal on the handle. She appeared to be puzzled and insisted that I had the knife. At last, apparently unconvinced by my assertion that I had lost my knife, she led me back to the building, and that was the end of my romantic adventure!

It was the custom for all the students to attend the Sunday evening prayer-meeting. The following Sunday I went along with the rest. At the close of the meeting as I was about to go the pastor called me aside and asked if he might not speak to me in private about an important matter. I loitered while the students were passing out, and I noticed that they looked back at me rather curiously. The doors had glass panels, and after all had passed out I saw some of the girls (oh, the girls!) looking through the glass.

The minister began to speak in sad and serious

tones. "In this country," he said, "it is not customary to carry knives." The moment he uttered
the word "knife" my mind went back to my lost
knife and to the incident of the walk with the young
lady. As he proceeded with words of counsel and ad-
monition, he used the word "stiletto" synonomously
with the word "knife." There appeared to be some
uncertainty in his mind as to just what it was, but
one thing was certain: I had a weapon and I was
an Italian. That was enough. All Italians carry
weapons and are dangerous creatures, according to
the common American belief. He assured me that
he harbored no ill feelings toward me, but he made
it plain that it was not a good thing to carry a
weapon and that since coming to the school I had
caused great disturbance by openly carrying a
"stiletto." He further stated that the girls (fragile
little creatures!) had refused to be in classes which I
was attending, while the boys had sworn that they
had seen me brandishing the dreadful weapon. "Unless you give it up," he continued, "you will be
obliged to leave school."

I was dumfounded and completely mystified.
True, I did actually have the weapon on me,
but of course I would not admit it! Would
you reader, had you been in my place? A tense
moment followed. Finally the pastor, to clinch
the matter, said that he himself had seen it a
few moments before, and for that reason had asked

me to remain. If I did not mind, he would at least like to look at it. The point of it was even then to be seen sticking out of my vest pocket, shining brightly against a blue silk handkerchief. I could deny it no longer. Taking hold of the lapel of my coat, he pulled it open, reached for the dreaded weapon and pulled it out. All was up with me!

It was an *aluminum comb*, conveniently pointed at one end to be used for manicuring, and not for carving out human hearts! It did look very much like a stiletto. I now saw through it all. How the good parson must have felt as he held it in his hand! So far as I know, no explanation was ever made of the matter, and to this day, I venture to say, some of my schoolmates still remember the dreadful days when they went to school with an Italian who carried a stilletto with which he intended to carve out hearts, both men's and maidens'!

A friend of mine once remarked that it would have been only fair if the authorities had made a statement relative to the true nature of the supposed weapon. For my part, however, I have always looked back upon that incident with much merriment.

The following incident I wish to narrate as illustrating how I first became aware of the American trait of open and fair play. It was at the beginning of the next school year, when as a "soph" I had begun to "feel my oats." As I have stated, Dr.

W. F. Berry was the president of the school. I consider him one of the noblest men it has been my privilege to know in America. I admired him very greatly and always listened very attentively to the brief addresses he used to make at chapel. These little talks were a great inspiration to me. They were so simple, so earnest and so practical that I understood almost every word of them. He generally spoke on matters of morality and good conduct, and in the course of his address he would frequently make use of the phrase, "a punctilious regard for the rights of others." This phrase had become a sort of byword with some of the boys, who would repeat it in making sport of the president. All this did not set well with me. In fact, it would so exasperate me at times that I had hard work to keep from striking some of the offenders. Next to me was rooming a "freshy" who took special delight in mocking the president, especially in my presence, because he knew how it affected me. He would frequently repeat the phrase in my hearing, and as frequently I did not hesitate to let him know how I felt about the matter. I stood it as long as I could. Finally, one day I assembled a group of "sophs" and led a raid upon the offending "freshy." Knowing me to be the leader of the gang, he naturally turned upon me with a vengeance. In the scuffle which ensued in his room, I reached for a pitcher and dealt him a blow upon the head, which broke the pitcher and drew blood.

I realized that I had made a bad break. Ashamed to look any one in the face, I remained locked in my room for three days, an upper-class friend bringing food to me. I was conscious that however justified I might be, this was a serious error. On the third day, Professor J. O. Newton, who in the president's absence from the school had charge of the administration, came to my room and informed me that it had been decided that I should leave the school unless I was willing to make a public apology. While I was really not very sorry for having risen in righteous indignation against the rascal, I agreed to make a public apology. That evening, supper over, the girls were dismissed from the dining room and the boys asked to remain. In a few words Professor Newton explained the situation and then gave me a chance to speak. It was a severe test for me; in all my life I had never had such an ordeal to face. But I stood up and frankly apologized. The boys responded with a great ovation which made it plain that I had touched the right chord. We were dismissed and the incident ended there.

But the way the matter had been handled impressed me greatly. In my home town, an occurrence of this character would surely have started a feud, at least among the boys. But here the straightforwardness, the fair play and the frankness which characterized the whole incident appealed to me as standards of conduct worthy of recognition and of acceptance.

I remained at the Maine Wesleyan Seminary for three years, during which time I passed through some unpleasant experiences on account of my foreign birth. A few students felt no hesitation in honoring me with a "dago" now and then, but this was not at all general. A far larger number showed a kindly and encouraging attitude toward me. There was one instance, however, in which a number of my fellow-students showed ill feeling because I was a "foreigner." This was during my third year in school, when the cast for the senior play was chosen. The "Senior Play" was considered the greatest event of the whole school year. Each year the cast was chosen by the faculty from such members of the senior class as were deemed most worthy. It was always considered a great honor to be so chosen. That year the "Merchant of Venice" was to be presented and the faculty was generous enough to assign to me the part of Shylock. This caused a furore among some of the seniors on two scores. In the first place I was not legitimately a senior. I had entered only three years before, but by dint of constant application and hard work I had managed to gain one year and was to graduate the following Commencement. This placed me in the

senior class by adoption, but not by inheritance.
Some of the seniors were very reluctant to adopt
me and threatened for a while to go on strike. The
second reason was that I was a "foreigner." Certain members of the class did not hesitate to let me
know how they felt about the matter. One boy did
not mince words: "You d...... dago! You have
no right to play that part or to be in the senior
play at all."

It has always been my philosophy, when anything
of this kind occurs, to take it as it comes, and dismiss it from my mind. In this case I gritted my
teeth, pulled the straps of my harness tighter, and
bending to the load, I resolved to prove whether or
not I was worthy of the honor which without my
seeking had been bestowed upon me. For the next
two or three weeks I worked almost continuously
night and day, until I had actually memorized every
word of the play. In view of the fact that I had only
begun to learn English three years before, I do not
myself see how I managed to do it. I am certain I
could never do it again! It was the urge of achieving
a goal for a definite purpose that drove me on.

My laborious task, however, brought its own re-
ward. It immediately won me the good will of my
fellow players. When we came to the first rehearsals
the majority of the participants, as usual, had not
learned their parts, while I had thoroughly memorized theirs as well as my own. Instead of their re-

senting this, they began to show a friendly attitude. As the rehearsals proceeded, and even on the very night the play was rendered, I jokingly acted as walking prompter, often putting into the mouths of the other players the words of their parts, saying good-naturedly: "Speak the speech I pray you as I pronounce it to you." I must own that the atmosphere had completely changed before we were through, and my fellow students showed an entirely different spirit.

The next issue of the school monthly had a flattering notice. I quote it here, because it so well illustrates my point:

"The character of Shylock deserves special mention. Mr. Panunzio took this part and it was certainly very finely done. The remark has even been heard from a critic in such matters that it has seldom been done better even by professionals.

"Perhaps too much cannot be said in praise of the way in which the acting was kept up to the end. Even when Shylock was not speaking he still kept the same appearance, mumbled to himself, cast looks of hatred on those whom he regarded as enemies and never allowed us to remember that he was Mr. Panunzio and not Shylock himself. The general verdict seems to be that this part was remarkably well done and deserves all the praise it can possibly have."

While in the outer world these praises were sounding, in my inmost consciousness something much
more vital was taking place. This was the first
real, tangible encouragement I had received since
that fatal night, four and a half years before, when
I had left the ship. As I reflected upon it, I began
to realize that, even with the serious handicap placed
upon me by my foreign birth and lack of language,
work would win; that I was, after all, the "captain
of my soul." I really began to believe, what I had
seriously questioned before, that if a "foreigner"
really tries to make good, recognition will come. I
further realized that with the better classes of
Americans, such as my teachers were, "a man's a
man for a' that." My participation in the play and
the favorable comment it had received were in themselves quite unimportant. And yet they would have
been significant in the life of any boy, and doubly
so in the life of a foreign boy. I had conquered
against tremendous odds, and for this I was chiefly
indebted to my teachers who had given me a chance.
And with the satisfaction that my first success
brought to me came my first desire to remain in
America and become a part of her.

While these thoughts were taking definite shape
in my consciousness, I had another entirely unexpected manifestation of the same principle of fair
play. At the State University at Orono, Maine, an
interscholastic oratorical contest is held yearly, to

which each of the twenty or more preparatory schools of the state of Maine send one delegate. Three prizes and two honorable mentions are offered. Our school had sent its delegate each year and had once captured the first prize, some fifteen years before.

When the faculty of the Maine Wesleyan Seminary came to choose its representative for the coming contest, to my utter amazement, the choice fell upon me. At first I did not see how I could possibly do it, but under the personal encouragement of my teacher in elocution, Miss Alma Gitchel, I finally took heart and set myself to what seemed a Herculean task.

For the next few weeks I worked untiringly in preparation for this supreme test of my school life. Two considerations held me unswervingly to my work. First the pride of the school was at stake, and I must represent her worthily. Second, here was an opportunity to prove to the public at large that though I was a "foreigner" I could play my part in life, were I given a chance. I had heard so much said against the "foreigner" that I had actually come to feel a sense of separation, and to assume an attitude of self-defense and a tenacious purpose to prove the worthiness of my manhood, independent of the accident of birth.

The time for the contest finally arrived and receiving instructions from the faculty, I started for

Orono. On the evening before the contest, a preliminary try-out was held and from the entire number of contestants, eight were chosen for the final contest. I had at no time been very confident; so I was somewhat surprised to find my name posted on the bulletin board the next morning as one of the final participants. The evening came and the contest was on. The chapel, seating some five hundred people, was crowded to the doors, and the interest was intense. I was fourth to speak. I gave the entire Court Scene from the "Merchant of Venice." From the moment I began, I was absolutely oblivious to the presence of the audience, lost in my supreme effort. It was a great moment in my life, the like of which I have experienced only twice since that evening.

The contest over, the judges withdrew and later returned with their decisions. One by one four of the contestants were called to the platform. As only three prizes were offered, I knew that I had failed. The chairman of the committee was the professor of Latin at the University. Solemnly he announced the awards, but instead of first announcing the first prize, he announced the two special mentions and dismissed the recipients from the platform. Then he announced the third prize and finally the second. When this was over, he stepped to the front of the rostrum. A tense moment followed. Amid a breathless silence, he made a few comments and then falteringly spoke my name and asked that I be escorted to the platform. The audience burst forth in tremendous applause. I sank into my seat. Something inexplicable gripped my very soul. My eyes became dim. It was not joy, nor sorrow, though perhaps a sense of triumph in a righteous cause. Here was success, and for it I was humbly grateful. At last I felt the shackles of suspicion and ill-will fall from me. I saw the triumph of Justice, not alone for myself, but for all who, like myself, had suffered untold humiliation.

I remained in my seat. The audience shouted, "To the platform, to the platform!" Some one escorted me up. I was awarded the first prize and a large pennant.

As the days passed and I realized more and more the significance of the event, I became thoroughly convinced that after all with America's best people, foreign birth makes little or no difference. Yet withal, there was an oppressive feeling of loneliness. I had no one in all this country with whom to share these little successes. Cannot one very much better bear the loneliness of failure than that of success?

Another matter connected with my school life deserves mention because it illustrates the inspirational methods of my American teachers in contrast to the coercion of my instructors in Italy, and the difference in results. At home I had left school as a direct result of not wanting to study mathematics. The bump which my tutor had made when he broke the ruler on my head, transplanted to the inspirational soil of America, had now grown so considerably that at Commencement I was able to win the only prize offered in advanced mathematics, for which several students had a neck-and-neck race.

At Commencement also I had an opportunity to compete with my fellow students in an oratorical contest. Every one thought that as I had used the Court Scene of the "Merchant of Venice" at the Interscholastic contest, I would also use it here. However, I realized that this would give me an unfair advantage over my fellow students, and I practically relinquished my rights in the contest. With an attitude of indifference toward it, I learned something else rather hurriedly, and was perfectly satisfied to lose the contest, rather than to seem to have capitalized my advantage over my fellow-students.

Before leaving this description of my school life, I must make brief mention of a trip I made to New York during the summer of my second year at school. I had heard of the Museums of Arts and of Natural History, and of the Cathedral of St. John the Divine in New York, the latter then in the course of construction. In the five years I had been in America, I had scarcely seen an edifice which stood particularly for Art or Beauty. I decided to go to New York to see them. I took the boat from Portland and as I did not have much money, I did not even purchase a berth. On reaching New York, I spent a day in the Museum of Art and one in the Museum of Natural History. I also visited the Cathedral on 110th Street. My monetary store being very meager, I lived on peanuts and milk during my entire stay, but I left with a feeling of great satisfaction and with a lasting impression of what I had seen.

In the autumn of 1907 I entered Wesleyan University, Middletown, Connecticut, one of three in a class of a hundred and twenty to be admitted without conditions. I had paid all my expenses and had $50 to start college on. All through college I had the sympathy and coöperation of the faculty. I paid all my expenses, partly through scholarships. I took part in minor athletics, represented the College on the Varsity Debating Team for three years, and participated in the various oratorical contests, winning some prizes. In 1911 I received an A. B., and in 1912 an A. M. In 1911 I entered Boston University School of Theology, intending to go into the ministry.

Two of my college instructors stand out above all others, though all with whom I came in contact did a great deal for me. One of these was Professor William North Rice. Professor Rice is one of those teachers of whom, alas! we have too few in our American colleges and universities. He has a remarkable ability to awaken independent thinking in the minds of his students. While his classes are not always large or popular on this account, there is in them an atmosphere of true learning and vigorous thinking. His course in Science and Religion was one of the milestones of my thought life, and one of the few courses I have found which puts more emphasis upon *thinking* than upon mechanical knowledge.

More than that, Professor Rice was a genuine friend to me. On many occasions I went to him for personal advice and he was never too busy to help me. I remember one occasion in which he gave me invaluable assistance. I had received news from Italy that one of my brothers, serving in the army at the time, had gotten into some kind of difficulty and needed my help. It was necessary that I send a cablegram, but I had no money, and did not know what to do. I went to Dr. Rice for counsel, and he not only spent three whole days in an effort to get my brother in Italy out of the tangle, but also insisted upon personally loaning me the necessary money for the cablegram.

To my much-esteemed Professor of English Literature, the late Dr. C. T. Winchester, I also owe a debt of lasting gratitude. He, too, had the gift of leading his students to do their own thinking.

Aside from that, he was to me the supreme American gentleman. Professor Winchester was chivalry and courtesy itself. The brusque and uncouth manner I had early learned to associate with Americans had no place in him. He was the very embodiment of a sturdy moral and religious character, and blended most beautifully with it was the most thoroughly refined and courteous outward manner. In the uniting of these characteristics, he was to me the American *par excellence*. From week to week I spent many hours in his study conversing on subjects of social as well as personal significance. These "conversazioni" stand out as the most inspiring memories of my college days. Above all else, I feel indebted to Professor Winchester for having introduced me to Browning, who has become to me an inexhaustible spring of vigor, power and optimism. Incidentally, I may say that I am happy to think I was able to submit this book to Dr. Winchester before his death.

All that my life in school and college meant to me, I cannot define. Far above what I acquired of knowledge and mental training, I had gained something of vaster significance: a new view of life. I had been brought up to believe manual labor a disgrace. Here in America I had earned my way through school and college; I had worked as janitor, tailor, woodsman, night watchman, mail clerk, and respectable people thought no less of me for so

doing. I even courteously but firmly declined to accept the aid of a lady who had become interested in
helping me financially. I hope I did not seem un-
grateful; such was not the fact. I was simply en
joying my independence to the full. The American
in me was unconsciously growing. I borrowed no
money until I was compelled to do so, and then I returned it as soon as possible. I took pride in my
toil and in being independent. "A new birth of
freedom," our immortal Lincoln would have said,
and with it came the consciousness that this was
possible only in America. This consciousness was
as invigorating as a newborn morning. It was
electrifying; it put new backbone in me; it broke
the shackles of petty conventionality; life became
a great adventure.

I have already indicated that it was during my
school and college days that I learned that after all
in America the accident of birth did not play a
great part in life. In fact, I felt sometimes that
my teachers and others favored me because I was
handicapped in language and otherwise. All in all,
my school and college life led me to really believe
that this was the land of true opportunity, and the
use of that opportunity has made a most valuable
contribution to my life and toward the growth of
what I call my American consciousness.

I SUFFER SERIOUS LOSSES

One lesson, Nature, let me learn of thee,
One lesson which in every wind is blown,
One lesson of two duties kept at one
Though the loud world proclaim their enmity—
Of toil unsever'd from tranquillity!
Of labor that in lasting fruit outgrows
Far noisier schemes, accomplished in repose,
Too great for haste, too high for rivalry.
                                        Matthew Arnold.

CHAPTER XI

WHENEVER I have recounted these experiences of school and college life, I have always betrayed my enthusiasm for American life and institutions. Some of my American friends, however, have objected to it. They say that had it not been for a series of mere accidents— as they call them—which led me to school and college, I might still be buried in the slums of some great city along with thousands upon thousands of non-English speaking people, and still be ignorant of the real heart of America. These friends point out that while a fortunate few, like myself, do emerge from the immigrant masses and write appreciative accounts of American life, there are millions who remain buried in cities within cities; and who, through no fault of their own, never even catch a glimpse of the true America; millions who never come in personal contact with a real American; who never see the inside of a representative American home. America, my friends say, is too busy to take any interest in them. too much concerned with the making of goods to care for the making of good Americans. She contents herself by delegating to a few hundred public school teachers the enormous task of transforming fourteen millions of "foreigners" into Americans, a task which belongs to the whole citizenry and which cannot even be touched by ten times the number of school teachers now engaged in it. America thinks that she can make Americans by coercion or by asking the aliens to attend a two-hundred-hour course on Americanization each year. For all these reasons, my friends point out, thousands upon thousands remain forever strangers to us and we to them, and therefore my glowing appreciation of what America is doing for the immigrant is far fetched. Then they also ask if there were not serious losses which I suffered while acquiring these new ideas of life.

Are my friends right? I fear they are. As to the losses I suffered in the meantime:

The first of these was the loss of that trustful simplicity which I brought to America with me. Then the persons I met were my friends. I believed in them, I believed their words, I trusted them. But beginning with the treatment I had received at the hands of George Annis and John Carter, I began to look upon Americans with a feeling of suspicion and distrust. My jail experience and the general attitude which people showed toward the "foreigner" gave me a consciousness of separation. I gradually came to believe that I was surrounded by enemies, and that my own attitude must always be one of self-defense. From trust and confidence I passed to suspicion and distrust; from believing in people to questioning their motives and looking upon every man I met with a big question mark in my mind. All this was in the very flower of my youth, and it has taken years of conscious struggle to overcome what was wrought into the fiber of my soul during the first two years of my life in America. Nor is this a condition peculiar to me, for the more I have come to know the immigrants in this country, the more have I found this attitude much more prevalent than the American public dreams. It may be that every man, whatever his nationality, goes through this period of disillusionment, but I cannot believe it is so acute, or that it comes in such a way or at such a youthful period as in my case.

A second distinct injury I suffered was the loss of my manners and the deep respect I had been taught for law and order. Those who would have us believe that environment has no effect upon life in its practical aspects at least, need to make a study of a limited group of immigrants, making records of their behavior in relation to manners and to respect for law and order at the time of their arrival, and again a year or two afterwards. The change is very striking.

I had been brought up on the "Galateo," a famous

book on good manners; I had been taught from childhood to conduct myself properly toward every person I met in life; to be chivalrous to women, respectful toward the aged, obedient to the law.

My early years in America attacked the very citadel of this respectful, courteous attitude toward life, and almost destroyed it before I was conscious of what was happening. And how could it have been otherwise? I came in contact only with the rough and the uncouth, with persons who knew no refinement of language, of bearing or of manners; who mocked order; who defied and openly broke the law; who ridiculed the old and infirm; who glibly talked of dumping the aged as you kill a sick dog and throw him away. Dignity had no place in life; liberty was license; vice was virtue. All this attacked the very heart of my early training, and the wonder is that as a youth, susceptible to the influences of environment, I escaped with as much of the real sense of the beauty and the dignity of life as I did.

In those early years I also came near losing my grip upon my health. I had inherited a vigorous constitution and when I came to America I was in the bloom of strength. I had lived the greater part of my life out of doors, especially upon the sea, and my every motion was one full of power and vigor. Aside from the minor ailments of childhood I had never been ill, nor had I ever had occasion to consult a physician. Since coming to America, however, life had made serious inroads upon my health. For years I was obliged to drive with all my powers in order to earn a livelihood and to compete with the world about me. I was forced to work not eight hours, but as much as fourteen and sixteen hours a day in order to keep my head above water. Then, too, there was the tension of continuous loneliness, of grief, of struggle, of abuse,—all of which attacked my nervous system, while the intensive rush of American life drove the propellers of the heart until they could scarcely stand more. During my first year of college I had to consult a physician for the first time in my life. I was suffering a general breakdown, and the only thing which saved me was a slowing down of my driving speed. But even then it was too late in a measure, and the loss in physical power which I suffered in the first five years in America will be felt for the rest of my days.

Perhaps even more serious than all else was the change which took place in my attitude in the matter of thoroughness and exactness in work. From earliest childhood one of the greatest satisfactions I had in life was that of doing things well. The art of painstaking and careful work seems to have been inbred in my very bones. Even in drawing or in making my little ships, it was instinctively exactness and beautiful workmanship that appealed to me. While at sea I used to spend hours making all kinds of articles of twine or rope, and at painting or carving, all of which demanded minute care and exactness. Although I had left school very early and had not taken well to books, whatever I did, I did with precision and thoroughness. Even during my first year or so in preparatory school my aim was always to be exact in my work even to the very last detail.

But I was caught, caught in the fast-revolving wheel of life about me. I saw everybody rush, yes, I *felt* the rush. Students placed a premium upon speed; upon getting through school as quickly as possible, no matter how. Those who could manage to complete their work in three years instead of four were considered the most capable students in school. Long before I came to realize that I was losing one of the choicest heritages of my life, one of the best things I had brought from Italy, I too had been caught in the whirlwind. It was not until I was almost through college that I became conscious of the loss I had suffered. Painful has been the task of retracing my steps in quest of what slipped away from me in the first three or four years of life in America.

Like myself, every immigrant brings something with him from his native land which is worthy of perpetuation, and which, if properly encouraged and developed, may become a contribution to our na-

tional life.   We would do well to afford to every
newcomer an opportunity to develop and to contribute the best which he has brought with him,
rather than to destroy it by any means, direct or
indirect.

I BECOME NATURALIZED

O joy! that in our embers
Is something that doth live,
That Nature yet remembers
What was so fugitive!
The thought of our past years in me doth breed
Perpetual benediction: not indeed
For that which is most worthy to be blest,
Delight and liberty, the simple creed
Of Childhood, whether busy or at rest.

   .   .   .   .   .   .
        Not for these I raise
        The song of thanks and praise;

  .   .   .   .   .   .
        But for those first affections,
        Those shadowy recollectioñs,
        Which, be what they may,
Are yet the fountain-light of all our day,
Are yet a master-light of all our seeing;
        Uphold us, cherish, and have power to make
Our noisy years seem moments in the being
Of the eternal Silence; truths that wake,
        To perish never;
Which neither listlessness, nor mad endeavor,
        Nor Man nor Boy,
Nor all that is at enmity with joy,
Can utterly abolish or destroy!

William Wordsworth.

CHAPTER XII

I T was in the spring of 1914, almost twelve years from the time of my landing in the United States, that I received my final naturalization papers. Why had I not become naturalized before? There were several reasons for the delay. In the first place, it took no small amount of moral courage to come to the point where I could honestly swear off allegiance from my native country and as honestly turn it to this nation. Now this was not due to the fact that I did not like this country, or because I did not value its institutions, its life, its ideals. Nor was it because I was so deeply attached to the political life of my native country that I could not bring myself to leave it. On the contrary, the cords which bound me to it were quite frail. But it was chiefly because of those wonderful, inexplicable tendrils which so intertwine themselves around our human hearts in our infancy as to make the country of our birth, the very village or hamlet in which we first saw the light of day, the one spot on earth around which cluster the sweetest of life's memories.

Go where you will, roam far or near over earth's diverging paths, still now and again those delicate tendrils pull at your heartstrings, and as long as life lasts, your mind will forever turn back with tenderness to the scenes of childhood, where you first became conscious of life.

Now in the face of this universal fact, how unkind, how cruel are the methods sometimes used in connection with our so-called Americanization program. Think of our saying to these foreign peoples, some of whom have been in this country for perhaps a brief period: Forget your native land, forget your mother tongue, do away in a day with your inherited customs, put from you as a cloak all that inheritance and early environment made you and become in a day an American *par excellence*.

This was precisely the talk I used to hear when I first came to this country. There was then as now, I regret to say, a spirit of compulsion in the air. "Either become an American citizen or get out," was in substance the attitude of certain people. But how was I to choose so suddenly? "Give me time for try," Thomas Daly makes an Italian say. I needed, as every immigrant does, this "time for try," to see whether I could honestly become an American. To speak frankly, what had there been during the first three or four years of my residence in this country which would have made citizenship at all attractive to me? Even had I wanted to be a citizen at that time, I could not have forgotten Annis and Carter, my jail experience, and all the rest that I had gone through. Had I not been sneered at as an undesirable "foreigner?" Had I not been maltreated, discriminated against, robbed, insulted, dragged to prison, despised? I grant you that I had suffered all this at the hands of the worst and very lowest elements of American society, but how was I to know there was any other? The struggle I went through in those early years in America in regard to my citizenship relation to her can only be understood by one who himself has had a similar experience.

It was during my senior year in preparatory school, however, that on the advice of friends I made a long trip to Portland, Maine, and took out my first papers, what the Italians call "the half citizenship." They have an idea that by taking out these papers they are sure of a certain amount of protection from the United States Government, while at the same time the act does not sever their legal tie with Italy, and puts them under no obligation to the United States. Perhaps something of this attitude led me to take out my first papers; at least I was in the state of mind of "well-it-won't-do-any-harm." By the time I was ready to graduate from preparatory school, I had really begun to have a desire to be a part of America, and gradually I came to feel that I would become a full citizen at the earliest possible moment.

Unfortunately, however, I left Maine and established myself in Connecticut while attending college. By my second year in college, the time had expired, and I was now ready to take out my full citizenship papers. But I soon discovered that to do this in Connecticut, I must have present two witnesses who would swear that they had known me for five years and that I had been in this country continuously for that period of time. This was not so easy a matter as might at first appear. Like every "foreigner" in this country, I was, comparatively speaking, a stranger. The only people I knew were either in Maine or somewhere equally far off; to bring them to Middletown, assuming that two such persons could and would leave their work and take the long journey in order to make me an American citizen, would have been a great expense. Later, when I was informed that I could have depositions made, I learned that these would cost me ten dollars, and ten dollars to a boy struggling to make his way through college was like a mountain of gold. There was no choice left but to let it go. I regretted this greatly, for by my senior year in college I had become deeply interested in American life and I wanted to take part in civic-betterment contests in our community.

The matter was still further complicated by my going from Connecticut to Massachusetts for graduate work. I still needed the two witnesses who had known me continuously for five years. How could this be? The friends I had known in Maine had naturally remained in that state and had no way of knowing whether in the interval of my attending college I had remained in this country continuously. On the other hand, persons I had known in college had known me at most for four years, and aside from one or two classmates whom I knew to be in the vicinity of Boston, I had no way of reaching them. It seemed as if I would finally be compelled to import two witnesses unless I was willing to let the matter rest indefinitely. However, if I did this, I might upon my graduation from Theological School go out of the state of Massachusetts, and the intricate round of difficulties would begin all over again.

In the spring of 1914 I made a desperate effort to get through the barbedwire entanglements which were keeping me from American citizenship. I found a college classmate who was willing to put in the time with me. He had by this time known me for about five years. There was another friend who had known me for five years, except for one month, during which period he could not tell whether or not I was in this country. All was off again; the inspector would not have it so, and in order to fill in the gap in my wandering residence over this country I had to import a third man who would swear that I was I and that during a given month I had been in this country. On that day four of us, all college students, spent almost the entire day in the antechambers of a certain office until his honor, the immigrant inspector, himself of Italian birth, would condescend to grant us a hearing. Worst of all, my poor pocketbook had to see a number of precious greenbacks emigrate, for it was necessary to feed my witnessing friends both for luncheon and dinner. But then I was growing accustomed to this exodus, for this was not the first time I had gone to his honor the inspector's office. It was a part of the price of acquiring my citizenship.

The absurdity of the whole process comes over me with full force sometimes and I have a hearty laugh over it. Think of a young man trying his best for several years to become a citizen in order that he may perform his civic duties, and then being hindered in every conceivable way. I recall the many times I had to go to the inspector's office; on most occasions we went on appointment, only to find ourselves still at the end of a long line at the end of an imperfect day. Every time this happened it naturally caused me embarrassment in that I was obliged to ask my friends to spend another day with me, not knowing whether the next would be any more fruitful than the last. The rudeness, the inconsiderateness of the officers was most disgusting; as

I faced man after man I wondered how they had been worthy of being placed in such important positions, where they were continually leaving bad impressions in the minds of those seeking the new citizenship. There is no place, it seems to me, where courtesy and consideration should be so constantly manifested as toward those "knocking at the gates" of the highest honor we can confer upon them. As I recall, there was anything but a courteous attitude shown throughout the whole process, from the Chief Examiner to the fat, red-nosed policeman at the door of the Court, who held us in a long line like cattle being led to the slaughter.

The moment I entered the courtroom, however, I felt the dignity of the step I was taking. Judge Morton of the District Court of Boston was presiding. He stood up, and amid the breathless silence of the court room, addressed us with that true simplicity, that deep earnestness and natural dignity which characterize a public officer who feels the responsibility of his office. His words were profound and inspiring. He spoke of what the step really signified, of the soul and not the shell of citizenship. As he did so, he gave me a new vision of what America would mean to me, and of what I could mean to America. As I stood before him, my only regret was that the larger majority of my "naturalization class" did not even understand the words he was uttering.

And so at last I was a full-fledged American citizen. I wonder whether my Roman forbears could have felt any more dignified than I did. As I reflect upon it, I am exceedingly grateful that I did not hasten into citizenship in answer to the cry of make-Americans-quick schemes; I am glad that I first became by real choice an American in spirit before taking the legal steps of becoming naturalized. I believe that I am a better American for it. And yet on the other hand, when I consider the endless difficulties I encountered in taking these legal steps, I wonder that more do not give it up as a bad job. If one with a comparatively good knowledge of the law and its methods finds it so difficult to go through the process of getting naturalized, how much more impossible must it be for those who, aside from having no knowledge of the law, do not even understand the English language?

STUMBLING BLOCKS
TO ASSIMILATION

This is the land where hate should die—
  No feuds of faith, no spleen of race,
No darkly brooding fear should try
  Beneath our flag to find a place.
Lo! every people here has sent
  Its sons to answer freedom's call;
Their lifeblood is the strong cement
  That builds and binds the nation's wall.

This is the land where hate should die—
  Though dear to me my faith and shrine,
I serve my country well when I
  Respect the creeds that are not mine.
He little loves the land who'd cast
  Upon his neighbour's word a doubt,
Or cite the wrongs of ages past
  From present rights to bar him out.

This is the land where hate should die—
  This is the land where strife should cease,
Where foul, suspicious fear should fly
  Before the light of love and peace.
Then let us purge from poisoned thought
  That service to the state we give,
And so be worthy as we ought
  Of this great land in which we live!

Denis A. McCarthy.

CHAPTER XIII

A s early as 1905, three years after my arrival in the United States, while I was still in preparatory school and before I had become naturalized or had even definitely decided to do so, I began to have a desire to do what I could to interpret America to the immigrant, especially to Italians, and an equal desire to interpret the life struggles of the immigrant to the American public. Young though I was, I realized that such experiences as I had personally gone through were more or less typical of thousands if not of millions of non-English speaking peoples in this country, and therefore I felt it my duty on general humanitarian grounds to participate in the work of mutual interpretation.

As chance would have it, that very summer I read a notice in a little religious weekly, in which an Italian Mission in Portland, Maine, asked for help from some one who could speak Italian. This appealed to my sense of social obligation, and although it was something of a financial sacrifice to give up

a more remunerative job, I answered the call and a
week or so later I was in Portland starting in on my
new work of helping the Italians of that city.

This was my first close-up contact with immigrants in America. From the very first I was much
impressed with the various needs of the people and
I saw many ways in which we could be of practical
service to the Italians of the city. I therefore made
plans to mingle with the people themselves, and,
regardless of whether they came to the religious
services we held, to help them in any way most
needed. I soon discovered, however, that this was
not what the authorities wanted or expected. Their
primary interest was to fill the little hall with
Italians at every service and to make just as many
"converts"—better proselytes—as possible. Some
of the workers gave themselves with great zeal to
this task, and they could not understand how I, with
my knowledge of Italian, could be so indifferent to
what they considered the most important phase of
the work. They were so zealous that they caused
very serious breaks in the home life of some of the
people. I recall one case where a young man was
cast out of his home by his parents because they
did not approve of his attending the meetings held
in our little chapel. He came very near going insane
under the strain. The American workers, however,
thought they had accomplished a great transformation, although the young man ultimately returned to

his parents and gave up the meetings. Thus early I came in contact with a class of Americans who think they can do anything they please with the immigrants and their children, when by causing friction and ill feeling in the home they are retarding rather than accelerating the work of assimilation and Americanization.

It was during that same summer that I saw in a very tangible way the results of the attitude which Americans in general maintain toward the "foreigner,"—another stumbling block to real assimilation. The Italian Government was about to open a sub-consulate in the city of Portland, and Signor V—— was assigned to the post of Vice-Consul. He was a man of fine and keen intelligence, tall and pleasing in appearance, and a gentleman in every sense of the word. He had a very attractive wife, and I believe, two children. In keeping with his position, Signor V—— naturally desired to live in a good section of the city. Knowing that I had an entree into some American circles, he asked me to help him find a suitable residence. I was glad of this opportunity, for this was exactly the kind of service that I cared to render. I assured him that we would certainly be able through some of our friends to find a desirable dwelling for him and his family. We started on our hunt, in the majority of cases Signor V—— accompanying me. We went to real estate agents, to friends, and to houses having the "For Rent" sign up, but everywhere we were turned down. It was exceedingly embarrassing for me, for I had assured my friend that in a brief 'time we would be able to find something for him. I could not understand what the difficulty was. There were some houses which the Vice-Consul could have had, but they were located in undesirable parts of the community and were generally unattractive. Finally I discovered that the chairman of the Committee which was in charge of the Mission I was serving had a house. for rent. Immediately I went to him, feeling assured that if anybody in the whole city would make it possible for the Vice-Consul to have a decent place to live in, he would. I called on him only to find that even the chairman of the Committee was not ready to rent a house to the Italian Vice-Consul. "And why?" I asked, almost in anger. "Because the neighbors would object to having an Italian (pronouncing the "I" long) next door to them." Then for the first time I understood what the difficulty had been. I was greatly chagrined and Signor V—— was greatly humiliated, and was finally obliged to locate in one of the worst sections of the city, in the midst of the Italian colony.

Now were this an isolated incident, it might not be worth narrating, but such is not the case. Any self-respecting immigrant could tell a similar story. I recall a prominent Italian physician in another city who had very much the same experience.

It seems easy to want to Americanize the "foreigner" at a distance, or to delegate the task to some one else, but when they get too near us, then the line is sharply drawn, not on the basis of true merit or the lack of it, but simply because one is a "foreigner." The result is seen in "Little Italies," "Little Polands," "Little Ghettos," and the like.

All in all, my first experience then at Americanizing and at helping the immigrant was far from encouraging. I returned to school in the fall in a very thoughtful, if not pessimistic, mood; especially as it had been a considerable financial loss to me. There was one result, however, which compensated all the effort and sacrifice. I was able to take back to school with me a young Italian, who started at the bottom and is now a minister in a Western state.

Upon entering college, once more I attempted work along the same general lines. It was at this time that I conducted my first Americanization class. This class was under the supervision of a special committee, the chairman of which was a manufacturer, and the general manager of his own factory. There were in the city some five thousand Italians, from whom was drawn the larger part of the working force of this particular factory of our chairman. We made every conceivable effort to get a goodly number of Italians to attend the class, but succeeded in securing only thirty or forty. We taught two main subjects: English and Citizenship.

In the latter course I endeavored to expound the principles of our democracy by outlining the history of our country. Now the pupils showed increasing interest in learning English, but showed a feeling of indifference, if not of hostility, toward our course in Citizenship. Fearing that there might be something wrong with the method I was using, or in the general approach I was making to the subject, one evening, putting all bools aside, I asked the men to tell me frankly just what was the difficulty. Among the pupils was a very intelligent young man, a graduate of a technical school in Italy. He started the discussion, pointing out that this instruction about democracy was all well and good as mere *talk*, but that it did not have any relation to real life. "Look at us," he said, "we work long hours for only a pittance, and see the treatment they give us in the shop. The boss kicks us and calls us 'd—— dagoes,' and *all that* in the shop of the man who gives you the money to run this class. . . ."

So far as those present were concerned, he had struck the right chord, for they all took sides with him, and a few had other interesting facts to reveal and accusations to make. This was all startling news to me. The statements and the complaints impressed me so deeply that I decided at the first opportunity to take up the matter as tactfully as possible with the chairman of the committee. who

was the employer directly involved in these charges.
I wanted to discover the real facts in the case.

One day I had occasion to go to the office of the
chairman on a matter of business, and among other
subjects, the conversation turned to the Americanization class. He first broached the subject by
making a complaining remark regarding the "lack
of interest in America on the part of your countrymen." This was my opportunity to discover how
far the men had any reason for fault-finding. I
had not fully believed all they said and was fundamentally in sympathy with my own and their employer rather than with them. I said something
like this: "Pardon me, Mr ——, I do not know
what more we can do to attract the men to the class.
We have tried every possible method to no avail. In
fact, from what the men tell me, our Americanization
work has no interest for them or any effect upon
them. They have criticised us and have complained
of our inconsistency; they have said that the ideals
of democracy which we are endeavoring to incul-
cate do not agree with the undemocratic way in
which they claim they are treated at their work.
Their attitude was so evident that one night recently
we put away all books and I asked them to state
their grievance. They frankly spoke of their difficulties. They know that you are personally sup-
porting my work; they say that they are being
ill-treated in their work and that I am in league

with you in hoodwinking them. . . . They say that
they do not receive enough wages to keep them in
decent existence; some of them say that a portion
of their wages is being taken from them weekly by
the 'boss.' Under these circumstances I find it
exceedingly difficult to teach them our American
principles. They shrug their shoulders and remain
completely indifferent, if not antagonistic, to all that
I try to teach them. I wish you would give me your
advice."

I had been perfectly calm in saying all this, and
really expected that we would talk over the matter
frankly. To my utter amazement Mr. —— became
incensed. The only advice he would give me was:
"Damn the dagoes, let them go back to their rat
holes"—and with that he was about to dismiss the
whole subject. For the first time in my life my
sympathies were turned toward the man under. I
said, "Mr. —— I am sorry that you take that attitude toward the matter. Please remember that
when you have trouble in your factory, when you
hear of labor difficulties of various kinds; when you
hear of I. W. W.'s and anarchism, of bombs and the
like, that it is the spirit back of your 'damn the
dagoes' that is responsible in no small measure for
these difficulties." The Americanization class ended
right there, for I could see no use in trying to do
anything along that line with such an atmosphere
existing around our work.

Realizing the futility of this kind of effort, I now turned completely away from it and became the pastor of a small church in one of the suburbs of Hartford, Connecticut. It was through a mere coincidence that I came to take up that work. It had been the custom for that church to have a pastor from the student body of Wesleyan University for several years. At the time of which I am speaking, the student-pastor, a friend of mine, was taken suddenly ill, and he requested me to supply his pulpit until he was well again. I went to the church, and, primarily because I had had some little success in platform work of which they had heard, the members were much pleased with my services. Time passed and my friend continued to be ill. In the meantime, we were enjoying success in the church, the services were well attended and a general feeling of harmony seemed to pervade. The time for conference came, and as it was uncertain how soon my friend would be well again, some one proposed that I be appointed as the regular supply.

For the moment it seemed as if an avalanche had been precipitated from a mountain top upon the church. The membership was immediately divided into two opposing camps, threatening the very existence of the organization. That I had rendered acceptable pulpit and pastoral service all acknowledged. Every one was well satisfied and pleased so long as I remained their *temporary* pastor, but it was inconceivable to a large part of the membership and especially to some of the official members, that I should become their *permanent* pastor. The difficulty was simply that I was an Italian. Those favoring my staying, however, won the point, and I was officially appointed and remained there two years, having a more or less successful pastorate. Before I left there, I had the satisfaction of hearing those who had originally opposed my staying say that they were in the wrong, and that after all the fact that I was of foreign birth should not have made any difference.

I continued to serve American churches for four years longer, one at North Cohasset and the other at Amherst, Massachusetts. During all this time, however, I still felt that I had an obligation both to America and to my native countrymen which called me to work in their behalf. At the same time, I felt a pride in that I had been able to assume some measure of leadership among Americans and I was not altogether anxious to return to work among the Italians.

It was at this time that an opportunity seemed to open up whereby I could still continue to work among American people and at the same time have a chance to express my inherent interest in the welfare of the Italian people. There was a church in a suburb of Boston, located in a downtown section, in which lived some twenty-five thousand Italians. The church in question had once been one of the most noted and prosperous; it had had some well known men in its pulpit and had taken great pride in its fame. But with the passing of the years the Italians had so invaded the community and the American constituency had moved away so rapidly that the church now faced a possible extinction. On the other hand, there was not a single religious or social organization ministering to the needs of the large Italian community. The authorities of the conference saw in the situation a double opportunity. If they could appoint a man to this church who could serve the small American constituency belonging to the church, and at the same time endeavor to do something for the Italians of the neighborhood, a very real and strategic service could be rendered. As I had served in Italian communities and had also handled some American churches, they thought I could do the very thing they were seeking to accomplish. Accordingly, they made their plans to assign me to the work. They had not, however, taken into consideration the weakness of human nature. The upshot of it was that the official body of the church could not "suffer to see this well-known church, or even a part of it, turned into an Italian church," and I was not appointed. The church continued to eke out an existence as before, while the numberless Italians within a stone's throw of it remained in their utter neglect.

MY AMERICAN
"BIG BROTHER"

The multitude of mankind had bewildered me and oppressed me,
And I complained to God, Why hast thou made the world so
wide?
But when my friend came the wideness of the world had no
more terror,
Because we were glad together among men to whom we were
strangers.
It seemed as if I had been reading a book in a foreign language,
And suddenly I came upon a page written in the tongue of my
childhood:
This was the gentle heart of my friend who quietly understood
me,
The open and loving heart whose meaning was clear without a
word.
O thou great Companion who carest for all thy pilgrims and
strangers,
I thank thee heartily for the comfort of a comrade on the
distant road.

Henry Van Dyke.

CHAPTER XIV

THERE is one man in all America who has, more than any one else, helped me to become an American, and who, by several years of unfailing and constant helpfulness has demonstrated, to me at least, what every American could do if he would, to help the "foreigner" to find his place in the American system of things. This man I have chosen to call my American "Big Brother."

The average American does not realize, perhaps cannot realize, how difficult it is for a young man of foreign birth to find his right place of self-expression and of service in American life. His background may be the very best, his American education the most complete, his desire to adjust himself to the life of America very real, but when the actual fitting-in process comes, he is face to face with almost insurmountable difficulties. If he is without parents in this country, as is often the case, he has been deprived of that parental guidance which is so much needed by every youth. If, on the other hand, he has his parents, he finds himself facing almost as great difficulties in that they so often do not sympathize with him in his desire to get into real American life. In either case, he has been deprived of that parental help which gives the native born many points of contact and makes it comparatively easy for him to find his way into an honorable and profitable profession or business. On the one hand, the youth of foreign birth finds himself confronting the inevitable difficulty of prejudice even on the part of good Americans, while on the other he is liable to be looked upon as a renegade by his own countrymen if he shows a desire to abandon the segregated life of immigrants and lose himself in the life of his new country.

Now it is quite clear from what has gone before that this was the case with me. And there was an additional factor which made it hard for me. Because of the experiences through which I passed, I was coming to feel that it mattered not how well educated I was, whether or not I was an American citizen, nor whether I did have an honest desire to become a part of America, I was still a "foreigner," do what I might, and so long as I was a "foreigner" no one particularly cared what became of me.

It was at this point that my American "Big Brother" came to play a part in the unfolding of the American in me. When we first met, he showed no particular interest in me; in fact, up to that time he had had a prejudice against Italians in general.

But as the years passed he watched, from a distance, my yearning to fit into the best of American life. In the meantime he had made a visit to Italy and returned with an entirely different attitude toward immigrants, and especially toward the Italians in this country. Before we met a second time I had chanced to write a brief paper expressing my convictions that only by offering the immigrant the best there was in America and by giving him an opportunity to contribute the best, can we as a nation ever hope to make the immigrant a part of us.

And now finding that I could not take up the work which I had intended because there was a distinct prejudice against the Italians and because the officiary entertained the horrible fear that their church might be turned into an Italian institution, I was now face to face with the problem of finding some other field of service. It happened that a certain institution in the North End of Boston was without a leader, and as friends had many times suggested that I assume its leadership, I now became favorably inclined to undertake it. Two forces, strangely contradictory, but ignorant of each other, now became serious obstacles. On the one hand, there were those of American birth who, as members of the committee of direction, claimed that only an American born could possibly assume the directorship of such an institution. But, as the community in which the social service house was located was very largely inhabited by Italians, some argued that my Italian background was a distinct advantage. I was sufficiently American in training and in outlook to safeguard American ideals, they claimed. But strange to say, this was the very reason, others claimed, why I should not be appointed. The constituency themselves, knowing something of my ideas about America, maintained that I was too much of an American and for that reason should not be appointed. I stood aside and laughed in my sleeve, realizing that neither side saw the incongruity of the situation: too little American on the one hand, too much of one on the other; too little of an Italian to one group and too much of an Italian to the other. Pathetic, to say the least! Funny, to say the most!

It was at this stage of the game that my American "Big Brother" stepped in. He happened to be a member of the committee of direction. I was told later by a third person that the real American in him, the American of the "square deal," of "fair play" arose in indignation. He stood up and insisted that birth should play no part in this, but intrinsic worth only. He hammered his Americanism upon the heads of the committee until they had to yield. As a consequence, they appointed me to the superintendency of the institution in question.

Now it was not the appointment itself which I cared about, but rather the spirit and the principle for which this man had fought. But even that incident in itself did not make this man so important a factor in my life. It was what followed as a consequence. As soon as I took up my work, he expressed himself in terms somewhat like these: "Count on me as your friend; your foreign birth makes no difference with me; call on me whenever I can be of help to you." As the months passed I found that I could really count on him; that he was my friend in reality, and was ready to spend his time in counselling one who was much in need of advice. Counsel, however, is as far as many people go in their relations to the immigrant. There are plenty of people who are willing to give abstract counsel, but are not ready to go to the limit of definite, concrete helpfulness to the stranger in a strange land. My American "Big Brother" went further, he was ready to put in time and energy in drawing closer and closer to me every day, and as he did so, I felt the fortifying encouragement of his companionship. Gradually he extended to me greater and greater privileges; he invited me to visit him at his home, not in a condescending spirit, but in a spirit of true brotherliness. We have sat about his fireplace times without number and discussed the problems of life. With him and his wife, a lady of true refinement and inborn culture, I have taken many rides over the wondrous country in the vicinity of the town where he lives.

We have gone together to concerts and to plays. We have worked and played together in his garden. He has introduced me to his friends, well-bred and cultured Americans, and he has done it all in such a spirit of true neighborliness, free from any condescension, as to make his friendship a source of constant inspiration and of practical help.

Nor was this interest born of some sporadic fad. He began the work of Americanizing the "foreigner" by showing him true kindliness and by making America seem a lovely thing and much to be desired, long before the present craze of the so-called Americanization movement was on. And as the years have passed I have come to feel more and more the power of his steadying influence. When I have passed through critical experiences he has stood by me as a sympathetic counsellor, a guide, a friend. When others have shown a tendency to say "foreigner" he has doubled his confidence. He has been practical, constructive, suggestive, sympathetic in his relations. And the beauty of it all is this: That until recently, when I expressed to him what he had been to me, he had done it all in an unconscious way and had not realized how fully he was exemplifying to me the true American. He is truly a man, the full measure of a man; lofty in his moral and spiritual ideals; noble in bearing and appearance; truer than steel. Above all, he has shown himself to be an American who so loves his country and who has such a belief in the fundamental power and genius of this nation, and who is so concerned with the unfolding of its true destiny, that he is willing to inconvenience himself, and instead of finding fault with immigrants, instead of pointing out the supposed inferiority of this or the other race, he has devoted himself in a practical way to the making of new Americans. I am certain that had it not been for my American "Big Brother" I would not have the deep-seated faith in America which is mine to-day.

I have gone somewhat at length into the description of the relation that this man played at a critical moment to the unfolding of the American in me and in evoking a deeper love for everything that is American, because of my ever-growing conviction that one ounce of this kind of treatment will do more to make Americans than a million pounds of the Americanization cure. All the classes in Americanization, all the Fourth-of-July orations, all the naturalization campaigns, would not have begun to do for me what this one citizen did. Americans are not made by simple formulas. They are born out of the embodiment of ideals; they are molded into shape by the hand of those who have mastered the art of treating men as human beings, whatever their color or nationality. When we fully realize this and act accordingly, then all the problems of the "alien" in America will largely vanish and our country will realize in a fuller measure a true assimilation of its varied people and a truer national consciousness and unity.

IN AN IMMIGRANT COMMUNITY

Lo, Lord, the crowded cities be
Desolate and divided places.
    .   .   .   .   .   .
Men who dwell in them heavy and humbly move
About dark rooms with dread in all their bearing,
Less than the flocks of spring in fire and daring,
And somewhere breathes and watches earth for faring,
But they are here and do not know thereof.

And children grow up where the shadows falling
From wall and window have the light exiled,
And know not that the flowers of earth are calling
Unto a day of distance, wind and wild—
And every child must be a saddened child.

There blossom virgins to the unknown turning
And for their childhood's faded rest are fain,
And never find for what their soul is burning,
And trembling close their timid buds again.
And bear in chambers shadowed and unsleeping
The days of disappointed motherhood
And the long night's involuntary weeping
And the cold years devoid of glow or good.
In utter darkness stand their deathbeds lowly
For which through the creeping years the gray heart pants—
They die as though in chains, and dying slowly,
Go forth from life in guise of mendicants.
             Rainer Maria Rilke (Trans. by Ludwig Lewisohn).

CHAPTER XV

THROUGH a series of circumstances, then, as strange as those which twelve years before had in a day snatched me away from it, I now returned to the very community in which I had first set foot on landing in America. But in those twelve years a revolution had taken place in my outlook on life. I had seen some of the best aspects of American life; I had come in contact with some of her best people; I had felt something of the high aspirations of a soul which has come to really understand American ideals. Naturally I would now see things in this community from a viewpoint which would have been impossible had I remained buried within its bounds all these years.

As I looked about me I said to myself: "Well, this is a real immigrant community, of which I have heard so much in the American world!" From the moment I first set foot in it, I began to be conscious of the tremendous difficulties which on the one hand confront America in her desire and efforts to assimilate immigrant groups; and which, on the other, are in the way of the immigrants themselves in their need, and often their desire, to become an integral part of the body American.

For one thing, here was a congestion the like of which I had never seen before. Within the narrow limits of one-half square mile were crowded together thirty-five thousand people, living tier upon tier, huddled together until the very heavens seemed to be shut out. These narrow alley-like streets of Old Boston were one mass of litter. The air was laden with soot and dirt. Ill odors arose from every direction. Here were no trees; no parks worthy of the name; no playgrounds other than the dirty streets for the children to play on; no birds to sing their songs; no flowers to waft their perfume; and only small strips of sky to be seen; while around the entire neighborhood like a mighty cordon, a thousand thousand wheels of commercial activity whirled incessantly day and night, making noises which would rack the sturdiest of nerves.

And who was responsible for this condition of things, for this crowding together? Were the immigrants alone to blame? Did they not occupy the very best tenements available, the moment they were erected and thrown open to them, even though at exorbitant rates?

Not only was all this true, but every sign of America seemed to have been systematically rooted out from this community as if with a ruthless purpose. Here still stood old Faneuil Hall, the Cradle of Liberty; here the old North Church still lifted its steeple as if reminding one of the part it had played in the Revolutionary War; here was Copp's Hill and many other spots of the greatest historical importance; not far away was State Street (old King Street), where the first blood of the Revolution was spilled; and here too, the spot where the Boston Tea Party, which had contributed so much to the making of America, had taken place. But while these monuments stood like sentinels reminding one of what this neighborhood had once been, now every last vestige of America was gone! All the American churches, homes, clubs and other institutions which once had graced these streets were gone forever; gone to some more favorable spot in the uptown section of the city, leaving this community to work out its own destiny as best it could. There *were* churches here, to be sure, Catholic and Protestant and Jewish, but they were representative of other than America; they were under the leadership of men who, consciously or unconsciously, stood for other than American sentiments and ideals. In the homes and on the streets no English language was spoken save by the children; on the newsstands a paper in English could scarcely be found; here were scores if not hundreds of societies, national, provincial, local and sub-local, in which English was not usually spoken and in which other than

American interests were largely represented. There were schools also in which the future citizens of America were taught in a language other than English. Here, when on a certain patriotic occasion, the American flag was raised a moment sooner than another flag, the person responsible for such a "crime" was nearly rushed out of the community. Above the stores and over those infernal institutions which are permitted to bear the name of "banks," the signs were mainly in a foreign language. In a word, here was a community in America in which there was not a sign of the best of American life. Had it not been for three well-organized and splendidly equipped social service houses and for the public schools, all of which consistently upheld American traditions and standards, this might well have been taken for a community in some far-off land.

Nor was this the whole story. Not only were all the constructive forces of American society absent from this community, but also some of its very worst features seemed to have been systematically poured into the neighborhood to prey upon the life of the people in their all too apparent helplessness. Here within this half mile square were no less than 111 saloons, not because the people wanted or patronized them to any great extent, but because saloons were needed for revenue, so it was claimed. If one section of Boston would not have them, was it not necessary that they should be established in

another? When Dorchester decided to turn out the
saloons from its precincts, as a matter of course,
additional licenses were granted to the "saloonists"
in North End. Who would care? Here in this
neighborhood were also 53 of the worst imaginable
institutions; poolrooms and bowling alleys, dance
halls and gambling dens, brothels and the like; again,
not patronized in the main by those living in the
vicinity, but chiefly by out-of- and up-towners.
Within or in the immediate outskirts of the community were also located eleven moving picture
theaters in which, according to an actual investigation, 95 out of every 100 films exhibited depicted
the lowest of practices, the vilest of scenes, the worst
of crimes; and to these houses were admitted children
and adults alike, the law notwithstanding. In this
community were committed some of the most
atrocious of crimes; once more, according to police
records, not committed mainly by the inhabitants
of the neighborhood, but by those who from every
unheard-of place came to this vicinity for their
misdeeds.

And while this was in no way a typical American
community, neither did it resemble Italy. No one
with the least amount of Italian pride in him would
want to boast that this was in any sense an Italian
community. In fact, more than one investigator
from Italy had pronounced it the very contradiction
of all that Italian society stood for; the pictures

which they painted would have made blush the worst descriptions given by American sociologists. For in this city within a city it was the misfits of Italian society who were "i prominenti" and held dominance; it was those who could "bluff it through," who were the "bankers" and the publicists; it was the unscrupulous politician who controlled things; it was the quack who made his money; the shyster lawyer who held the people within the palm of his hand.   True, there were some persons who could really be classed as Italian gentlemen, but they were few and could easily be counted on the fingers of both hands.   Again, here were thrown together by the hand of fate the humblest elements of Italian society, who though leading a peaceful existence, still were representing and perpetuating in a miniature way the interests of a hundred petty little principalities and powers in the limits of a single community. Here a thousand trifling, provincial and local animosities and controversies were brought together and fostered in a way that out-Babeled Babel.   This conglomeration of folks would have been as much an anomaly in Italy as it was in America.   The best of all that Italy stood for was not here.   You might hunt in vain for the least sign of that sense of the beautiful, that refinement, that leisureliness, that culture, that courtesy of manner so typical of Italy and the Italian.   A sad and sordid picture this; it may displease some, I fear, but it is as true as a correct mental camera could photograph it.

But why paint it at all? Because as a native of Italy and a lover of all that is beautiful in her, I should like to have every Italian and every lover of Italy see it in its true sordid colors; look at it until his fixed gaze would reveal to him that this is not representative of the real Italy; look upon it until he shall come to hate it and every other community like it as I hate it. Because as an adopted American I should like to see every American lover of America look at this picture and every similar picture in all its ugliness, consider the causes that gave it birth and keep it alive; until beneath the intensive and penetrating gaze a determination shall be born in every heart to destroy such communities throughout the country by cutting the roots that give them life.

And yet, strange as it may seem, I came to love the people of the community as deeply as I came to abhor its communal life; I came to love them for the simplicity of their characters and lives, for their hidden capacities, for their jocundity, for their sincerity of purpose, for the beauty of their home life, for the indomitable courage with which they faced the most untoward circumstances in which they were placed.

It was the children who first beckoned to my

affections. I came to love them as I saw them, through no fault of their own, separated in thought and life from their parents, and equally separated from all that was America. I loved them as I looked upon them at play in the littered streets. I loved them as I saw them in a thousand unconscious ways express their yearning for the beautiful, the true, the lovely, and all that child life so yearns for.

I recall how my heart went out to them one day, as I entered the community with a cluster of roses in my hand, which I was intending to take to my institution. As I passed down the street the children gathered around me as they once gathered about the Pied Piper of Hamelin Town:

"There was a rustling that seemed like bustling
Of merry crowds jostling and pitching and hustling;
Small feet were pattering, wooden shoes clattering,
Little hands clapping and little tongues chattering;
And like fowls in a farmyard when barley is scattering
Out came the children running.
All the little boys and girls
With rosy cheeks and flaxen curls,
And sparkling eyes and teeth like pearls,
Tripping and skipping, ran merrily after,"

as they shouted one after another: "Please, Mister, give me a flower." How else could it be, with their love for the beautiful as expressed in flowers, and so seldom permitted to see it! I had no roses left when I reached my destination.

And I loved them for the songs I so often heard them sing. One evening, standing upon a roof, my attention was drawn to little voices singing, their clear notes rising above the tumult below. I listened. From one direction came the strains of the most popular song of the time: "It's a Long, Long Way to Tipperary, but my heart's right there." Over to my right I could hear the music and could almost distinguish the words of "Santa Lucia." While from a third direction I heard a baby voice singing in strains supremely sweet:

"O Little Town of Bethlehem,
How still I see thee lie;
Above thy deep and dreamless sleep
The silent stars go by;
Yet in thy dark street shineth
The everlasting light;
The hopes and fears of all the years
Are met in thee to-night."

It almost seemed as if the sweet little voices and the baby hearts were conscious of yearnings unrealized.

I came to love the children, the boys and girls, as I saw them bend beneath heavy loads in their efforts to help their parents in the struggle to make a living. Often I saw them in after-school hours as they went out to gather wood for the hearthstone fire. One afternoon I saw what seemed to be a pile of boards walking on two little human legs and feet. I touched the boards and gently stopped them. Looking under them I saw a baby face, a boy not over seven years of age. And one evening as the sun's last rays were kissing the water of the Charles River, I saw a boy pulling a load too heavy for his small shoulders, up the steep incline toward the State

House on Mount Vernon Street. Brave little hearts these, that shared the burdens with those who could not bear them alone, in their efforts to eke out an existence.

I came to love the mothers of this community, more lonely than all the rest, yet putting up brave faces against the most tremendous odds. I remember one especially, a widow. I had heard of her need and called upon her one day. I knocked at the door. Back came the sound of baby voices, the pattering of baby feet. The door did not open. I knocked again, then tried the door; it was locked. The baby voices and the baby feet were locked in while the widowed mother was out in search of bread for her brood. I returned at night. In the desolate room in which she lived a small kerosene lamp was burning. It was dark and damp and dreary. She told me her story. Left alone with three children, she had struggled long to keep them alive, earning nine dollars a week washing dishes in a restaurant, paying five of it for her one room, and locking her children in it while she went out each day to her toil. One of her children had succumbed, the baby. It had died only a short time before and had been buried in a nameless grave. As she told her story back to my mind came the picture of her struggling soul as painted by Daly. Had he known this woman's sorrow? It seemed as if he was uttering her very words:

"Da spreeng ees com'; but O da joy
Eet ees too late!
He was so cold, my leetla boy,
He no could wait.

"I no can count how many week,
How many day, dat he ees seeck;
How many night I seet an' hold
Da leetla hand dat was so cold.
He was so patience, O so sweet!
Eet hurts my throat for theenk of eet;
An' all he evra ask ees w'en
Ees gona com' da spreeng agen.
Wan day, wan brighta sunny day
He see, across da alleyway,
Da leetla girl dat's livin' dere
Ees raise her window for da air
An' put outside a leetla pot
Of—w'at you calla—forgat-me-not.
So smalla flower, so leetla theeng!
But steel eet mak' hees heart a-seeng:
'O now, at las', ees com' da spreeng!
Da leetla plant ees glad for know
Da sun ees com' for mak' eet grow;
So too, I am grow warm an' strong.'
So, lika dat he seeng hees song.
But, ah! da night com' down an' den
Da weenter ees sneak back agen,
An' een da alley all da night
Ees fall da snow, so cold, so white,
An' cover up da leetla pot
Of—w'at you calla—forgat-me-not.
All night da leetla hand I hold
Ees grow so cold, so cold, so cold.

"Da spreeng ees com'; but O da joy
Eet ees too late!
He was so cold, my leetla boy,
He no could wait."

And I remember a mother who late one night knocked
at my door, as if in a frenzy, and sent me out in
search of her boy, the boy of her love, the boy who
had gotten beyond the power of her control. Sad

indeed was the picture I saw long past the midnight
hour when I came back to her home without her boy.

I came to love the fathers too, many of whom
were putting up a brave battle to make a living for
their families. One I remember well. He had been
in this country for fifteen years. He had done all
in his power through the years to eke out an existence. He had five children, all born in America.
One day he was telling me of his struggle when he
broke out: "If only I had no children I would go
back to Italy. I was poor there, but even poverty
is better in one's native country. But I cannot take
my children back to my native land. They were
born here, they are Americans, they have been
brought up in this country. Work as I may, I find
it ever more difficult as I grow older to make a
living for them." He was a man of fine sensibilities;
his heart was breaking beneath the load.

For all their beauty, their simplicity, their
patience and endurance, for all their native intelligence and sensibilities, for all their sense of pro-
priety and their law-abiding tendencies, for the
wholesomeness of their lives, for the immaculate
characters of the mothers, for the unconscious aspirations and loveliness of the children, I came to
love these people.

It was into this community and into this condition
of things that my American superiors sent me. As
they gave me instructions, what they did not utter

seemed to say: "Go quickly, encompass the earth, go in a day and 'Americanize' and 'Christianize' them." They sent me into a building which was anything but representative of the American conception of orderliness, cleanliness and beauty; and anything but suitable for a work of uplift and inspiration. The building was very old and had been used for every imaginable purpose, from a monastery to a storage house, and was sadly in need of repairs. It was a monstrosity, dark, dirty, damp, ill-lighted and poorly ventilated. Forgetting that even the humblest Italian has a love of the beautiful deeply ingrained in his consciousness, my superiors thought this building altogether adequate for the work of transforming all these people in a day from "heathens" to "Christians" and from "foreigners" to full-fledged "Americans." When we came to actualities, we found it difficult to make our constituency believe that this was a church, or even an institution. Moreover, the building had been acquired in an indirect way from certain Catholic interests, and this created a feeling of antagonism from the very outset toward it and toward the institution housed in it. Under the urge of the impulse to speedily "Americanize" and "Christianize," the work had formerly been conducted in such a manner as to arouse the antagonism not only of the people of the community, but also of those persons who should have been its strongest allies, the leaders of the social service institutions to which I have already referred. Antagonisms had been aroused and conflicts created which were conducive to anything but the best social welfare of the neighborhood.

Again, my American superiors kept ever before me the *quantitive* idea of things. To them it was not a question of how solid a foundation we were laying, or how far we were benefiting the community and its people in those unseen ways, through inspiration and amelioration; their one idea was "How many?" Nothing seemed to please like a crowd. How it was made up, what the objective might be, what the outcome in terms of social life, were secondary considerations, if considerations at all. I often heard it said: "We must make a good showing." *Showing*, not *doing*. This tremendous pressure was felt not only by our institution, but by others as well. It gave rise to a competitive, duplicating and wasteful system of things. For one thing, the triangle of those little, almost insignificant institutions known as "Protestant Missions," of which ours was one, was on the one hand ever competing for the negligible Protestant following of the community, and, on the other, so inter-related as to form a vicious circle. The services at these missions were held at different hours. One Sunday I attended them all and found the same constituency, meager as it was, swelling the ranks of all three.

Later, by mere accident, I learned that seventy-five per cent of the membership of one was enrolled on the books of the second, and thirty-five per cent on the books of the third. One might say that no harm was done by this triple alliance; yet loyalty was not being fostered thereby, and what perhaps is more significant, the American superiors of each of the three missions were content with their apparent "much serving," when in reality it was the same one-course dinner served up three times. Even more interesting than this was the discovery that on the occasion of the opening of the third mission, which had recently taken place, the pastors of the other two had come to the rescue of the new and enterprising pastor by a "professional" understanding with him, whereby he could count on their membership until such time as he had built up one of his own, and in that way make a good "showing." In the meantime, the people went on pretty much their own way, practising their Old World customs and habits as if nothing American were within a thousand miles of them.

The fact was that this community, by the will of the American people and that of the immigrants, or more correctly speaking, in the absence of the constructive will of any one group of people, was leading a life almost completely separated from the life of America. What this separation of foreign-born people of any nationality signifies is fully illustrated by the remarks made several years later by a leading American. Though they describe an entirely different community and deal with a different racial group, yet the fundamental principles are so much the same that I quote it here.

It was in the autumn of 1919, at the beginning of the far-famed Steel Strike. I had been assigned by a certain institution to go down to the Pittsburgh region and endeavor to discover at first hand some of the facts underlying the whole situation. I went from village to village where trouble was brewing in its most acute form, and at last I reached Monessen, Penn. On approaching the little city, upon the hill across the river and overlooking the town below, I saw two men with guns strapped to their shoulders and with binoculars before their eyes, carefully scrutinizing the scene in the distance. As I passed over the bridge leading into the town two armed guards, one standing at each side of the bridge, looked me over as I passed. In the city itself men were walking two by two silently watching every passerby. Here and there were special deputies, some of them negroes, their badges prominently displayed. I was informed that the night before, under the cloak of darkness, two thousand American men, under the lead of a major, a veteran of the World War, had gathered on the plateau overlooking the city to

receive instructions and to drill, as if to prepare for
a new war. I was told that in this community lived
some 16,000 foreign-born people, mainly of Slavic
origin, and that all this preparation was being made
on their account. The whole aspect of the community reminded me very much of villages close up
to the firing lines, which I had seen in Italy not long
before.

I had a letter of introduction to one of the leading
men of the town. This man was one of the oldest
residents of the city and had seen it grow from
nothing to what it was then. He was a business man
of good standing, the president of a bank, the editor
of one of the papers, and a loyal American citizen,
whose sympathies were first and last with America
and with law and order. The strain of the situation had been so intense that he had been ill
in bed from it. Learning of my errand, however,
he courteously came down and gave me an interview.
In answer to my questions as to the causes underlying the whole situation, this was what he said:

"The present situation, sir, can only be met by
armed force. I regret to say this, but it is absolutely true. I am ashamed to think that such a
thing should ever have been necessary in our town.
Ten or even five years ago we could have done anything we wished peacefully; a simple method of education would have prevented all this. But we are

primarily to blame; we have forced a feeling of separation upon these people. We needed them for the growth of our industries, we wanted them to come and we did see them come to us by the hundreds. But we refused to admit them to our civic and social life; we gave them no access to our societies, our schools and our churches. We called them "undesirable aliens," we forced them to segregate into sections of their own and to organize into separate groups in which only their own language is used. First they organized for the purpose of giving expression to their social cravings, and then those very groups served as centers of self-defense when we showed antagonism to their segregated life.

"When first they came to us they were as innocent as children; the better elements of our community neglected them. Radical leaders, taking advantage of this, had their day and did anything they pleased with these people. We only looked on, laughed at their doings, and called them 'Hunkies.' Now they have us by our throats. Only last Sunday, 'Mother Jones' addressed a great crowd of them on the outskirts of the town. They have been raised to a high pitch of excitement. They have been taught that by means of this strike they can take possession of our mills and our town. Our lives and our property are unquestionably in great danger, but the fault is ours. If we suffer, we do so for what we ourselves have left undone in the years gone by."

STILL MORE OBSTACLES
TO ASSIMILATION

The Stranger within my gates,
  He may be true and kind,
But he does not talk my talk—
  I cannot feel his mind.
I see the face and the eyes and the mouth,
  But not the soul behind.

  .   .   .   .

The Stranger within my gates,
  He may be evil or good,
But I cannot tell what powers control—
  What reasons sway his mood;
Nor when the gods of his far-off land
  Shall repossess his blood.

                    Rudyard Kipling.

CHAPTER XVI

THIS is only a part of the problem. Not only are immigrant communities left pretty much to work out their own destinies; not only are there a thousand unsolved problems arising from the conditions which are allowed to exist in them; but there are characteristics inherent in the very nature of the immigrant people themselves which must be considered if a true assimilation is to be effected.

One difficulty lies in the fact that the vast majority of immigrants come to this country after reaching the age of mental maturity, and it is a question how far they can be changed in their outlook. I recall one case which illustrates this quite forcibly. This was a man about thirty-five years of age when he came to this country, and forty-five at the time of which I write. Born in a little hill town of Sicily and having lived his whole life in that primitive village, he had naturally adopted the habits and customs of his environment, which had created his whole general outlook upon life. Subsequently I had occasion to visit that little hamlet in the heart of mountainous Sicily, where hardly a sign of modern civilization exists to-day. As he had been a "contadino" in his native village, his development had naturally been very limited. In this country he had first worked in a factory and later as a janitor.

His manner of dealing with his family was decidedly brutal and domineering. His wife and children were almost as beasts in his sight. He loved them as a warm-hearted Italian can love his children, but he never allowed them to use their own initiative or to express their best selves in any way. He used to beat them mercilessly. Their jobs were decided upon by him; their earnings were his, and in many other ways their lives were wholly circumscribed by him. It was not that his children deserved such treatment; on the contrary, they were well-behaved young people, but they naturally did not look upon things as their father did.

As I felt a special responsibility toward his children, for reasons which I need not state, frequently I would talk to him, explaining to him what were the American ideas of home life and parental direction and control. He would listen attentively and patiently. Sometimes it seemed that he was actually getting the new idea, and I would think for a little while that he would really change his actions. But the very next day I would discover that he had again by a flogging forced his dogged

will upon his boy or his girl, and had done exactly
the opposite to what I thought he had understood
and promised to do. The fact was that he was beyond the power of Americanization in these as in
many other essentials. He spoke English quite well,
he had become an American citizen, and was very
proud of his citizenship; but he had passed the age
when a man absorbs new ideas or forms new habits.
How far such a man can be truly Americanized is a
serious question.

This same inherent difficulty of inadaptability to
American life is also present in the educated men
and women who come to us from non-English-speak-
ing countries. Quite often illiterates and those who
possess little education are much more pliable and
susceptible to American influences than educated
persons. Several young people who fall into the latter category have come under my observation at one
time or another. One was an extremely bright and
attractive young man, a graduate of the University
of Rome. He showed every possibility of making a
good American. After much argument he was persuaded to enter an American school. He mastered
English in a remarkably brief period, so much so
that he even wrote and published some poems in
English of no inferior character. But he was continually ill at ease, maintained a drifting attitude,
had no definite plan of life, and felt that his training
and ability were not sufficiently appreciated in this

country. I viewed him at close range then, and as I have thought of him in after years, I have realized that there was a fundamental difficulty in him which is typical of many of his kind. His mental outlook was fixed long before he came to America; his conception of life had already reached its highest development, and it was beyond his power so to readjust himself as to really appreciate American conceptions of life. The last I heard of him he had left school, had given up his idea of an American education and was head-man in a shoe-shining parlor in Portland, Maine.

This difficulty obtained also in the case of another, a Sicilian. He was a man about thirty-five years of age. He had been in this country four years, was a graduate of a technical school in Sicily, and was a thinking and versatile man. He had a well-balanced mind and was anxious to fit into the life of America. He had taken out his "half citizenship" papers, was attending night school faithfully and showed in every way a desire to become an American. He would often come to visit me, and would pour out his soul in pitiful pleadings, asking for help in finding his place in life. My friends and I did all in our power to get him into a good position, only to find him helpless in his effort to readjust his mental outlook to the life and thought of this country.

It is even more serious to find this lack of adaptability among those who have come to this country while comparatively young, but who have remained in an immigrant community during the period of their unfolding. This is best illustrated by the experience we had with several young people whom we succeeded in sending to school. My own experience, as I look back upon it, convinces me that the all-important factor which set me upon the road to Americanization was my having been entirely separated from all immigrant community life during the period I was attending school and college, and thus having an opportunity to get a real taste of American life. So I reasoned that if a number of promising young men and women could be led to leave the immigrant community I have described and go to some preparatory school, we would have a concrete example of what might be accomplished in the way of assimilating the younger generation. By a process of selection, we set out to discover a few young persons who showed promise and a desire for an education. During the first year of the experiment we selected four and encouraged them to go to school. To make this possible, we interested a few friends in supplying part of the necessary funds. Then securing the consent of the parents and making all arrangements, we sent these young people to some of our best preparatory schools.

By the time of the Thanksgiving recess, it became apparent that things were not going so smoothly as we had hoped. For one thing the parents had made it plain that they did not like the plan. They complained that it reduced the family income to such an extent as to cause them privation. This was not true, as we had made sure to select such young people as were not really needed by their families. The parents further claimed that too good a knowledge of English on the part of the children was not desirable, as thereby they would lose their love for the mother-tongue. Again, they maintained that the absence of the children from the home for even so brief a period, would cause a spiritual breach.

On the other hand, it was evident that the young people themselves were ill at ease in their new environment and away from their old associations. They did not like the food, the rooms, and they thought it humiliating to work for part of their expenses. One girl became almost ill crying for her home; one boy said he could not live away from his parents; another stated his parents needed his earnings, and so on. The fact was that the parents had continually written the children to return, and this had added to their I-want-to-go-back feelings.

By an almost superhuman effort, we managed to keep them in school. I personally visited them at the schools and tried in every possible way to persuade them not to give up the fight. By Christmas time, however, it became apparent that they could hold out no longer. The old life was calling, calling them. Two of them dropped out at Christmas, the remaining two held out until the Easter recess and then back they went to their old life.

Undaunted by this experience, we tried it again the following year, taking an entirely new group in order to really test the experiment. We sent out six young men this time. The result was practically the same. We attempted a half-way method by encouraging some to go to school near Boston so they could return often to visit their relatives. The outcome was no more encouraging, and at this writing, out of a total of nine young people whom we thus attempted to awaken to a larger life, only two are still persisting in an effort to secure an education. The most discouraging feature of the entire effort was to see these young people perfectly satisfied to go back to their old environment, and lead their old mode of life. They even became the most staunch opponents of American ideas and ideals. The Old World had too much of a grip upon them and it was futile even to attempt their assimilation into a new and larger world.

Nor does the problem stop here. Even with the small children, there are almost unconquerable difficulties to surmount as long as they are born or brought up in immigrant communities such as I have described. Can we really ever effect their assimilation so long as they live in these strange little worlds? Here again my experience in Boston affords an illustration.

A woman in our constituency had three children, two boys, one seven and the other five years old, and a baby girl. She was a widow and was having a bitter struggle to eke out an existence. She came to me one day requesting that I interest myself in placing the little girl in a nursery, and the boys in a kindergarten or school. I proceeded to make such arrangements at the public school, when one day she came to my office and broke out crying. I could not make out what the trouble was. After she calmed down, I asked her to tell me the difficulty. After evading several questions, she finally said: "Please don't send my children to an *American school*, for as soon as they learn English they will not be my children any more. I know many children who as soon as they learn English become estranged from their parents. I want to send my babies to a school where they can be taught in the Italian language." Here, then, is at least one reason why it is possible for many schools, other than public schools, to exist in America, where languages other than English are used almost exclusively. And even though we stifle our emotions as we see a mother plead for the privilege of keeping her children always hers, we still must consider how we can manage to bring them into a knowledge and appropriation of American life and thought in the face of such an attitude.

The fish vender on the street corner near historic North Square gave me another illustration when he abruptly stopped me one day and said: "Please tell me what is the trouble with my little nephew?" He was a boy of about thirteen years of age and just that afternoon had caused trouble in the street. I asked him what the difficulty seemed to be, and he said, "Why, that boy was a model of obedience two years ago when he came to this country. He never thought of uttering a disrespectful word to any of us and especially to his mother. He was always home early at night, and would always kiss his mother before going to bed. But since he has been here he is getting worse and worse. We can't manage him now. He is disrespectful at night, he gets home when he pleases, he uses language more vile and profane than that used by a hardened tough. We don't know what to do with him. Do the schools in America teach boys to become bad? Will you help me to send him to jail?" I explained that it was not the school's fault entirely, nor the boy's, but that the situation arose from the conditions of life existing in the immigrant community.

Still his question is very important: "Do American schools teach boys to become bad?" Is it not true that as the immigrant child goes to school and learns English he becomes estranged from his parents, becomes disrespectful and causes trouble in the home and the community? And is it not also true that as these children get a smattering of American ideas and ideals they become so independent as to be uncontrollable? And is it not this class, and not the immigrant himself, who fill the juvenile courts and swell the number of our delinquency cases in houses of correction?

It is and it will always remain a problem with which American society has to deal as long as we do not have a better method and a better system of distribution of our immigrant population, and as long as we permit these cities within cities to exist apart from the main body of our American society. Immigrant colonies as they now stand are impenetrable citadels, whose invisible walls no amount of Americanization can batter down. Some of the factors in the situation are inherent in human nature, others could be done away with by a proper adjustment in our educational system and by means of a proper distribution of the immigrant population.

I GO TO JAIL
ONCE MORE

On the curb of a city pavement,
'Mid the ash and garbage cans;
In the stench and rolling thunder
Of motor trucks and vans;
There sits my little lady,
With brave but troubled eyes,
And in her arms a baby,
That cries, and cries, and cries.

She cannot be more than seven,
But years go fast in the slums;
And hard on the pains of winter
The pitiless summer comes;
The wail of sickly children
She knows; she understands
The pangs of puny bodies,
The clutch of small, hot hands.

In the deadly blaze of August,
That drives men faint and mad,
She quiets the peevish urchin
By telling a dream she had—
A Heaven with marble counters
And ice, and a singing fan,
And a God in white, so friendly
Just like the drugstore man.

Her ragged dress is dearer
Than the perfect robe of a queen!
Poor little lass, who knows not
The blessing of being clean.
And when you are giving millions
To Belgian, Pole and Serb,—
Remember my pitiful lady—
Madonna of the Curb!

Christopher Morley.

CHAPTER XVII

I HAVE gone somewhat afield from the narration of my own personal story. The considerations which have occupied the last few pages, however, constitute a distinct part of the development of the American consciousness in me, and for that reason I have dwelt somewhat at length on them. We now turn to another strictly individual experience which also has its social bearing.

The incident occurred in the summer of 1916. I was still in North End as superintendent of the institution referred to. The house was located in the very heart of the most thickly settled section of the community. In midsummer, when the air is hot and there is scarcely a breeze stirring, it is almost unendurable to live there. The nights are especially insufferable, and one can see the people, almost naked, lying about the streets or on the fire escapes and the roofs.

In order to bring what little relief we could to the life of the people, and especially to the children of our neighborhood, we conducted a summer school consisting of classes in the manual and domestic arts, and of giving the little folks many outings and picnics. We also had sent to us from many parts of New England an abundance of flowers which we distributed daily to the children. So fond were they of flowers that we always had difficulty in keeping order when the time came for their distribution.

This work filled a great need in the lives of these little children. In order to get closer to the problems of daily existence, I lived in the community with these people. But it was somewhat nerve-racking. Therefore, it was my custom each evening to leave the neighborhood completely and go for a stroll through the Common or on the Esplanade in order to get a breath of fresh air and a little re-invigoration. One Sunday in mid-August was what New Englanders call a "scotcher." Not a breath of air was stirring and the temperature, well up toward a hundred degrees, was charged with excessive humidity. The streets of our little immigrant city were fairly covered with people too warm even to laugh or to talk. They just simply lay about trying to hold on to the thread of life. The moans of the little children would have awakened pity even in a stony heart.

In the late afternoon I started for my usual stroll. I reached the Common. The ground was fairly covered with people trying to get a breath of air. Some had spread newspapers on the grass and were relaxed full length upon them. Here and there was a mother with her brood of little children, the little ones rolling on the grass and the mother trying to rest. From their dress and appearance, it was clear that most of these people were from our community.

I was walking diagonally across the historic grounds, when to my left I saw people rising quickly and running in a semi-circle. As when human beings, suddenly finding themselves driven before a flood of lava or water, stand bewildered before the approaching danger, not knowing which way to turn; so this mass of humanity was suddenly arising from the ground and moving rapidly, scattering in every direction. I walked toward the rising tide and soon discovered the cause! Three policemen with clubs in hands were driving the people away. I stood still for a moment watching the pitiful scene. Here and there a man had fallen asleep beneath the oppressive heat, and was not aware of the approaching storm. One of the policemen would walk up on tiptoe and with his club strike the sleeping man a blow on the soles of his feet, causing a sudden awakening and a scream of fear. Here and there mothers hastily gathered their broods and ran before the approaching stream of human beings. As I stood still and watched the scene, hot indignation arose within me. I would have remonstrated, but remembering how futile it is to reason with such men, I turned away with disgust in my heart, and wondering whether Boston's citizens would stand for such treatment of its people. I asked myself: "Is this truly Boston Common?"

Two weeks passed, during which time I called the attention of some friends to what had happened. The scene remained very vivid before my mind's eye. It was now the 8th day of September. Toward evening, turning away from my usual toil, I again started for my evening walk. I strolled leisurely uptown where, at seven o'clock, I was to meet a friend in front of the State House, and to go to dinner. As I passed Park Street Church, near the northeast corner of the Common, I looked up at the clock tower and compared the time with mine. It was exactly 6:40. Walking to a seat in front of the Shaw Memorial, facing the State House, I sat down for a moment of rest and meditation, awaiting the coming of my friend. I was scarcely seated when a patrolman walked up and brusquely ordered me to "move on." I have learned that it is wise in the vast majority of cases to obey such orders, however much I may not see the reason for them. In this case, however, it seemed absolutely unreasonable. I had just that moment reached the seat; I was all alone; I was not obstructing traffic nor causing a disturbance of any character. In order to avoid any possible misunderstanding, I told the officer I had just arrived and was there to meet a friend. I even took out my professional card and offered it to him as a means of identification, in order to prove that I was a peaceful citizen. His answer was: "I am not here to argue; I ordered you to move on and I'll give you just three minutes." With that he stepped away and, leaning against a stone wall near by, waited for the three minutes to pass.

I did some rapid thinking in those three minutes. Something distinctly American rose up within me. Was I possibly infringing upon any one's rights? If so, why did not the officer inform me? Was I loitering or trespassing? Was I where I had no right to be? I saw no sign or indication that such was the case. Was it not best for me, anyway, to "move on" as I had done in so many similar cases? Was it not better that I should obey, however unreasonable the command, and for the sake of my name and reputation "move on?"

Just then the scene which I had witnessed two weeks before on these very grounds loomed before me in bold relief. It seemed as if I could see again the rising tide of humanity, and the policemen hitting men with their clubs, and the mothers and children driven before them like beasts. That settled my doubts. I could see no reason why I should be compelled to move, and I was now willing to suffer whatever might come for the sake of the principle involved. Had not others done the same on these very grounds long before my time? Perhaps through what I might endure, Boston's citizens might come to know some of the things which went on in their liberty-loving city, and which from their homes in the uptown sections or in the suburbs they never see.

The three minutes expired; the patrolman walked up to me quickly and taking hold of my shoulder began to handle me roughly. "Gently, Officer," I said, "please place me under arrest first and let the law judge, before you deal me any rough treatment." "Oh, is that it, freshy? All right, come along with me. You are under arrest," was his answer. Just then two young men happened to pass by. I requested the officer to allow me to take their names as witnesses. This he refused to do. I managed, however, as the officer dragged me along, to hand one of them a dime and give him the names of two prominent citizens of Boston, friends of mine, with the request that he call them up and notify them that I was under arrest and needed their help. At 6:50, exactly ten minutes from the time that I had passed the Park Street Church, according to the records at the police station I was under arrest and the patrol wagon had been summoned.

I was taken to the Joy Street Jail, and I

had my first ride in a patrol wagon. On the
way the patrolman who had arrested me did not
miss the opportunity to inform me, "We'll see
now, freshy." Knowing there was nothing to be
gained by it, I made no answer. On reaching the
police station, I was led to the chief officer's desk
and there, while an officer stood on each side of
me, I was asked a number of questions: my name,
my residence, my profession, etc. "What is this
man charged with, officer?" asked the sergeant.
"Loitering and obstructing the traffic, and refus-
ing to obey the officer's order to move on." I made
no answer. I was informed that I could go out on
bail if I could furnish a $50 bond and would appear
in court on the following day. I had about $25 on
my person, and I offered this and a check for an
equal amount which I would make out to whatever
name was desired. I had my check-book with me.
This was refused; it was necessary that I produce
the amount in currency, I was informed. As I could
not do this I requested that I be allowed to telephone
some friends to bring the necessary cash. I was
informed that I could not be permitted to do so.
Accordingly, as there was no way out of it, the two
guards, who had in the meantime stood by as if
watching one of the worst of criminals, marched me
to a cell and locked me up. I offered no objection,
for there was nothing I could do.

The cell in which I was placed was about four

feet wide by eight feet long. It had no window or other means of ventilation. On one side, close to the wall, was a wooden settee, running the whole length of the cell. There was no covering of any kind upon it. Near the bars which faced the corridor a comfort receptacle was set into the settee. From all appearances and from the awful odor that arose from it it was evident that it had not been cleaned for a long time. The walls were covered with all kinds of lewd pictures. In the next cell a woman was locked up, who apparently was a master of the English language of a certain shade. Under these circumstances, and with the oppressive heat, the outlook for the coming night was not at all rosy. I kept calm, however, hoping that some friend would somehow come to my rescue.

About three quarters of an hour passed when, entirely unexpectedly, a man whom I had not even thought of appeared on the scene. He walked up to the cell bars and said in excitement: "For Heavens sake, man, what are you doing in there?" He was as white as a sheet. I laughed. He was the pastor of a nearby church, whom I knew well. When the patrolman who had made the arrest had heard me state my name and profession, he appeared to have realized that he had overstepped the mark. He went to the church of my friend, called him out from his prayers—he was just beginning a prayer meeting—

and hurriedly told the story, saying: "For God's sake come and bail him out." My friend was thoroughly angry. He turned to the sergeant and asked why he could not have kept me in a waiting room until some one could come to bail me out. Finally he produced the money and I was about to be released from the cell, when two other close friends appeared on the scene. The young man had done the telephoning. It seemed for a moment as if there would be some other arrests, in the police station itself, if more calm was not shown on the part of my rescuers.

In about an hour from the time of my arrest I was at liberty once more, none the worse for the experience. In fact, it was a most valuable one to me. I had not only seen what actually happens when a man is arrested, I had also seen the inside of an ordinary cell and had learned many things which were enlightening.

The next morning I appeared in court. From the very first I had not the shadow of a doubt as to the possible outcome. I was certain that I had not at any time uttered a word or acted in a manner which a respectable citizen would be ashamed to own. I was called up to the witness stand and in response to the request of the judge I narrated the entire incident pretty much as narrated here. In fact, I have taken it almost verbatim from notes which I made at the time. I was acquitted; the officer received a reprimand, which I was told was exceedingly severe.

I felt it my duty to let the public know the details, not only of the personal incident, which in itself was insignificant, but of what lay back of the whole story, especially the scene which I had witnessed only a short time before on Boston Common, and which really had been responsible for my being willing to undergo arrest.

The Boston press, always on the alert, had already given some notice to the occurrence. Without my knowledge, some papers had, on the very night of my arrest, printed an account of it with a photograph, but thanks to the Boston *Post*, which took a decided interest in the matter, we were able to conduct a publicity campaign with the object of calling the attention of Boston's citizens to some of the conditions and abuses which were being permitted to exist in the city. People took an interest in the matter and I received several letters expressing appreciation for the stand I had taken and more especially for the motive lying back of it. One letter urged me to go a step further and bring suit against the city for false arrest, but I would not consider this. After all, it was not a matter for which the city or its authorities were responsible, so much as the attitude and conduct of an officer of the law.

Perhaps the deepest significance of the whole incident, in so far as its personal effect upon me is
concerned, was that it gave me an even deeper conviction and more profound belief in the power of the
American courts to settle matters justly. Of course
I was not then, nor am I now, unaware of the possible weaknesses of the courts of justice in this
country, but I was willing, and am now, to take my
chances on receiving a just judgment from an
American court, more than perhaps from any other
American institution. This was the third time I had
been before an American court and the third time
that the equanimity and the integrity of American
judges was impressed upon me. I believe that
America can well afford in all matters of law to let
the immigrant have access to the courts of justice,
rather than to leave them to the mercy of any other
institution.

I sincerely wish that I could say as much for the
policemen with whom I have come in personal contact. Of course I realize that we are dealing with
an entirely different class of men, and yet I am
certain that much could be done with the personnel
of the police force of our country, especially to im-
prove their methods in dealing with the immigrant
groups, by a simple method of police schools such
as France is establishing. This was the third time
in my experience in this country that I had come
in personal contact with policemen. I had found

two of them rough, inconsiderate and almost inhuman; the others had been generous, helpful and decidedly human, and had demonstrated to me, a stranger in a strange land, what a friend to the "foreigner" a policeman may be if he but will. I regret that this is not more often the case, for the policeman holds a most strategic place, as a representative of official America, in the life of an immigrant community.

My own personal experiences as a prisoner, as an observer in police courts, as a defender in some cases, have led me to believe that our police system often seriously retards the assimilation of the immigrant and arouses an antagonism in him which it is almost impossible to penetrate.

An incident which came to my personal attention some years later, connected with the Steel Strike of 1919, will illustrate what may often be seen in the police court, and will give to the American reader an idea of the feelings of the immigrant when he finds himself dealt with in the manner described.

In a certain police court in Pittsburgh a number of Russians and Jugo-Slavs were daily being tried, in early morning sessions, for alleged disturbances in connection with the Strike. It had come to my ear that certain abuses were being perpetrated. In the interest of American fair play I decided to be present one morning and see how far these charges were or were not true. Several cases came up for a hearing in which I did not detect any injustice in the sentence.   Police court over, I saw a young Russian go up to the sergeant and pay his fine of $10. The fine paid, the young man requested of the officer a writ of transfer, stating that he desired to appeal to a Judicial Court, not because of the fine he had paid, but because he had not had a chance to defend himself in the police court.   Thereupon I saw the burly policeman, a giant compared to his victim, take the young Russian by the shoulder and give him such a sling as to land the latter in the hall some ten yards away, and almost off his feet.   That was the only satisfaction he got for requesting the right to appeal—a fundamental American right!

MY AMERICAN
PHILOSOPHY OF LIFE

Where the mind is without fear and the head is held high;
Where knowledge is free;
Where the world has not been broken into fragments by nar-
    row domestic walls;
Where words come out from the depths of truth;
Where tireless striving stretches its arms toward perfection;
Where the clear stream of reason has not lost its way into
    the dreary desert sand of dead habit;
Where the mind is led forward by Thee into ever-widening
    thought and action,—
Into that heaven of freedom, my Father, let my country awake.
                                        Rabindranath Tagore.

CHAPTER XVIII

MY AMERICAN PHILOSOPHY OF LIFE

DEAR BROTHER VINCENT:

In asking me to outline what changes in my thought life I directly attribute to my residence and experience in America, you have asked me a question which has been very much in my mind of late, especially since my recent contact with Italian life and thought. I fear I cannot give you what I know you would want without going somewhat into detail, but since you have requested it, I will furnish it to you.

I wish you would bear in mind, however, that such changes in my outlook upon life as I am about to describe, are in no way typical of what occurs in the mental awakening of the average immigrant in America, be he an Italian or a native of some other country. The fact is, as you know, that mine has been an extraordinary opportunity and privilege to come in contact with the best people in America; whereas the vast majority of what are here called "foreigners" remain pretty much segregated, living very much the same life, in thought as in other ways, as they lived in the countries from which they originally came. If my experience has any significance at all, it lies in the fact that it shows what a transformation in the thought-life of the foreign groups could actually take place, if in some way or other they had access, as I have had, to the real life of America.

Then, too, you will remember, as you read on, that the outlook which we boys had in Italy does not necessarily represent that of the average Italian in Italy. Many young men had greater educational opportunities than we, and for that reason their outlook in our day or to-day may be much broader than ours was. I do think, however, that all in all, my outlook upon life was in a measure representative of the thought life of Italy, and especially of that section of Italy in which we were brought up and received our education. Do you not think so?

I attribute most of the changes of which I am about to tell you, some of them actual revolutions in fact, to my having come in contact with the best thought-life of America, especially during my educational career. It is of course conceivable that some of these changes might have taken place had I grown to manhood in Italy, and especially had I gone to the University, as originally planned for me. But that is a matter of conjecture at best. Moreover, it is quite certain, you will grant me, that with father's death I would no more have gone to the

University than you or our other two brothers have.
Then, too, I think I have a pretty good criterion
that my thought life would not have changed fundamentally had I remained in Italy all these years,
in what I gather is your outlook to-day, and that
of our brothers. You have all come in contact with
the larger thought life of our native country. At
any rate, what I shall here outline for you is what
actually has taken place, regardless of any possible
changes which might have been effected in my life
under favorable circumstances in our loved Italy.
All this, you understand, is for the purpose of comparison and without any derogatory thought in
mind toward my old outlook.

Now as to the changes themselves: The first of
these was the gaining of what I might call a *mobile
and free attitude toward life.* In each case I will
tell you just how the change occurred. When I
first came to this country, I clearly remember how
deeply I was impressed by the adventurous, free and
easy attitude which people here take toward life.
Now you will grant me that life in our little city, as
throughout all Italy, is pretty much static. It is
a thing seldom heard of for families, or parts of
families, to move from one city or village to another.
Generation after generation live in the same place
and it never occurs to them that they might benefit
by going to another part of Italy to live, or even
to a nearby town or city. Our own family, for in-

stance, has lived in Molfetta for many generations. Like every other person who leaves our native city, even father, when he went to the university, kept *looking back* to his native city with the idea solidly inculcated in his mind, of establishing himself in Molfetta. It may be of interest to state that in my own experience *the one thought* which was uppermost in my mind for years after I left home, was that, however far I might go or however long I might stay, some day, some fair day I was *coming back* to Molfetta. You may recall how father used to repeat to us Latin and Italian sayings to the effect that the old was always preferable to the new because more sure. Do you remember this one? "Via trita, via tuta" (the beaten path is the safe path), and also: "Chi lascia il vecchio e prende il nuovo, sa che lascia ma non sa che trova" (he who leaves the old and takes the new, knows what he leaves but does not know what he hath in view). Now that was exactly the conception which controlled my thinking when I reached America. It is true I had taken some decidedly new paths, but I had done it in partial defiance, unconscious of the old conception, but not in obedience to the new conception which displaced the other after I had lived in America several years. It is also true that thousands of our people leave Italy every year for the utmost parts of the earth, but it is not in obedience to a definite attitude toward life, but as a matter of necessity, and they are always reluctant to leave the old and approach the new, and eagerly look forward to the time when they can *go back*.

From my very first observations in America, I find exactly the contrary to be the case. People have no scruples, it never occurs to them to have any scruples, about leaving one city or one section of the country and establishing themselves in another. I am speaking now of representative Americans, for of course there are exceptions. Even here they have a proverb which says: "A rolling stone gathers no moss," but the better thought of the country answers: "Who wants to be mossy?" The mental outlook is one of adventure and free movement. I remember how deeply it impressed me to find a family which had for years lived in southern California living in the State of Maine on the Atlantic Coast, some three thousand miles away. I was also dumfounded to learn with what ease a young man born in Canada and living for several years in Maine, decided almost in a day, to go to live in Boston, where he has become a lawyer. It is not an extraordinary thing to find whole families pick up bag and baggage, in an hour, as it were, and go to live in another part of the country, as if it were nothing at all.

When I first became conscious of this freedom of movement on the part of American people I used to think it was perhaps due to the recklessness of some individuals. But the longer I live here, the more I feel that it is one of the outstanding characteristics of the people as a whole. Life for them is a great adventure. They do not hesitate to leave the old for the new, especially if they see in the new an advantage of any kind or degree.

It took me five years to recognize in this freedom of movement a possible benefit, and to put it to a test in my own life. It was precisely with that end in view that I made the great jump, as I thought in those days, from Maine to Connecticut, a comparatively short distance, as distances go here. I had a good opportunity to go to the University of the State of Maine, but I chose to make an experiment by going to college in far-off Connecticut. And as the years have passed I have come to recognize a mobility, a freedom of movement in life, as a distinct advantage, and thus the first great change has taken place in my conception of life. I have adopted it as the first plank, I might call it, in my American philosophy of life.

My next change was in the matter of *my attitude toward the customary*. In this connection do you not recall how carefully we were taught to follow custom? Do you remember how our adult relatives were kept in constant worry and fear that they or we children might overstep, in ever so minor a way, the bounds of custom? Our lives were circumscribed by the consideration as to whether this little act or that was customary. Father used to say to us, you will recollect: "Usus loquendi!" (custom speaks or commands) whenever he wanted us to do a thing which we did not want to do, or vice versa. That was the most effective way of bringing us to act according to usage and was the most imperative thing he could say. I believe we seldom thought in terms of right or wrong of the deed, but rather the customary or non-customary. Am I not right?

This was the second great lesson which I learned in America,—to pay attention rather to *the right or the wrong* of an act, than to whether or not it is customary. Now I would not give you the impression that people here disregard custom. Not at all. I find that here the individual is left pretty much to his own judgment and that his first consideration is not custom so much as whether a thing is right or convenient or advantageous. I think that the first thing that brought to my attention this characteristic of American thought in a striking way was a quotation of three lines from the English poet, Tennyson, which I used to hear quoted by public speakers:

> "The old order changeth, yielding place to new,
> And God fulfils himself in many ways,
> Lest one good custom should corrupt the world."

With that as a starting point I came to realize more and more that custom is not altogether an unmitigated good, and that subservience to it, perhaps I should say *to it alone*, is oftentimes a source of corruption and evil. And as this realization took definite shape in my consciousness, I also recognized it as a distinct characteristic of the American way of looking at things.

Not unlike this was the change which took place in my thought-life regarding the *opinions of others.* I do not recall any of father's teachings on this point, except that he used to say something about consulting an "old sailor" about the weather. If he ever gave us any instructions in regard to this, it has entirely slipped my mind. Anyway, he himself was so independent and so free from the snare of other people's opinions that he could not have said very much about this. I do not mean to use the idea of "consulting" as synonomous with "regard for the opinions of others." You will see that there is a very clear difference between the two concepts: one refers to a person's seeking the advice of another, whether or not he follows the counsel given; the other has reference to that obnoxious practice so prevalent everywhere of "sticking one's nose in another's business," as Americans say, and trying, with or without reason, to impose their opinions upon others. The idea of freedom from the opinions of others differs from that of freedom from custom, in that the latter is a general force, while the former is the definite expression of one person regarding the doings of another.

Now I think you will call to mind how people we knew in our boyhood days were actually slaves to this kind of practice; how they were continually worrying over what this or that person had said or might say. As a direct result of that early influence, I had acquired a habit of doing the same thing. In my first few years in America I carried it to such an extreme that I was continually changing my course of action to suit what this man or that man had said. This caused me not a little trouble, and has had a more or less detrimental and permanent effect upon my life. Possibly some of it was due to the inexperience of youth, yet I believe it was more deep-seated than that. At any rate, I attribute my present attitude to my contact with America.

One of the first sayings I learned in America, and which has had a profound influence upon my thought life was this. Some one, apparently taking exception with Shakespeare's famous dictum, "Conscience makes cowards of us all," remarked, "It is not conscience, but cowardice that makes slaves of us all." That is, it is not our deepest convictions nor what our inmost selves dictates that makes us cowards, but rather *our fear of what people will say* if we put into action our inmost convictions. In powerful lines, which I find myself repeating often, Browning, in his "Paracelsus" has expressed, indirectly and in a positive sense, this same idea:

> "Truth is within ourselves; it takes no rise
> From outward things, whate'er you may believe,
> There is an inmost center in us all,
> Where truth abides in fullness. . . .
> . . . . and to Know
> Rather consists in opening out a way
> Whence that imprisoned splendor may escape."

In quoting these lines, I generally substitute the word "live" for "know," and thereby I have in concrete form another plank in my American philosophy of life.

Another striking change which has taken place in my way of looking at life and which is directly due to my residence in America is my conception of *real* as contrasted with what I might call *inherited worth*. In this connection, it will doubtless come to your mind as it does to mine, how deeply we were impressed in our youth with the thought that our ancestors were great people and the thought was often implied, if not expressed, that their greatness was enough to make us great, or at least to give us an honorable place in society and assure us our livelihood. We were to reap not what *we would sow*, but what *they had sown*. I was particularly a slave to this conception of worth on account of my bearing our hero grandfather's name and of being told, times without number, that I was to be great, not because of any particular merit of my own, but because I was the direct representative of our revered ancestor. I lived in that consciousness throughout my youth and sincerely believed that it would make a comfortable and worthy life possible for me.

On my arrival in the United States, that idea was as powerful as ever with me. However, it did not take me long to discover its utter inconsistency with the life of people here. They have no family trees of which to boast, no class distinctions to speak of, no nobility or caste of any kind, and they make no talk of ancestors, with the exception of a few who claim descendence from the "Mayflower Pilgrims." These last are publicly ridiculed for making such boasts. In my early residence here, I used often to boast of the fact that I was descended from such a line of people as ours. My listeners would look at me in a blank and uninterested manner, offering no comment or praise. This would annoy me and I would say to myself: "Stupidi." But as I learned more and more of the simple unostentatiousness of American life, I came to love it, and I realized that it was after all the very highest attitude to take toward life. They place a value here on a man's *own worth and character*, be he the descendant of the humblest peasant or of the highest lord. Here poor men have the chance to, and often do, become rich; here a person of the humblest birth, like the immortal Lincoln, may even become president; here a person of modest circumstances is intrinsically on a par with the rich; here all men are equal, at least they have an equal opportunity to get on in life, according to their ability and ambition.

Here people also emphasize *progression in worth;* not what a man has been, not even what he now is, but what he aims to be. This thought is characteristic of the best in America. It was first brought to my attention very forcefully by two lines of Lowell, an American poet. I saw them only once on a motto in a book store one day, about five years after my arrival in America. They bore such a contrast to my wonted mode of thought that though I have not seen them since that day I still remember them as if I had read them to-day. These are the lines:

> To change and change is life, to move and not to rest,
> Not what we are, but what we hope, is best."

In those lines I saw then, as I have seen more and more in the years that have followed, what I consider one of the most outstanding characteristics of American thought-life; its mobility, its spontaneity, its freedom coupled with an ever-expanding life, the foundation and the aim of which is *real worth,* and not a consideration of what I have termed one's *inherited worth.*

This leads me to the next distinctly American characteristic of life which I have come to adopt as a part of my philosophy and practice. I refer

to the *practicability* of American ways. That my
conception of life should have been idealistic, in fact
ultra-idealistic, might well have been expected. For
not only is the temperament of our people, as of
all the Latin races, one of idealism, but I had, as
an individual, been brought up, perhaps more than
the rest of you in our home, in an atmosphere sur-
charged with idealism. I need only to refer again
to the ideal goal which grandmother had set before
me. And as you know, father himself was so
idealistic that he was continually finding it difficult
to face the realities of life; he lived so much in the
realm of the ideal that, with all his powers, he died
comparatively poor.

When I first reached this country I busied myself
so much with high and lofty ideals that I suffered
considerably, so far as the practical side of life was
concerned. I was continually dreaming great
dreams of what I was *going to do* some day, but I
never busied myself with even beginning to do the
great things, or even with making practical plans
as to how I was to actualize them. I made much
of conditions. "*Some day*," I would say to myself,
"when conditions become favorable, I will do this
or that."

The one thing which above all else focused my
attention upon the futility of looking at life in this
way, was an incident which took place while I was
working in Boston. One day we had a meeting of

the committee of the institution of which I had charge. I made a short talk in which I outlined the things I was planning to do as soon as conditions were right. I thought I had made a splendid impression. At the close of the meeting, he whom I call my American "Big Brother" walked out with me. As we were quite intimate with one another, I naturally was expecting a compliment from him. To my surprise, however, he turned on me rather sharply, and said, "I am tired of hearing you talk about your dreams, of what you are *going to do*. Your ideals are all right, but what about the practical working out of them? Why don't you 'get down to brass tacks' and tell us what you have *already done?*"

I was dumfounded and I confess it hurt me. But from that day I began to observe life as I saw it around me in America. I gradually came to the conviction that one of its outstanding characteristics is its practicability, not the less idealistic, but rather a *practical idealism*. Perhaps I have had a greater fight in striving to acquire this element of my American philosophy of life than any other. I am profoundly grateful that I have been privileged to see the difference and to have had a chance to strive for its realization in my life.

To another friend I am indebted for my awakening along another line. One day this friend and I were passing through a western city. Stopping at a hotel, we went up to the desk to make reservation for the night. The clerk informed us that the house was "full." In keeping with my Latin temperament I immediately started to argue, in the hope of making the clerk find us a room, when my friend turned away in disgust and said: "I ask no favor of any man." It hurt my pride, I must confess. All our teachings, you know, were to the contrary; the entire environment of our childhood had taught us that the asking and granting of favors was a great part of life. Favoritism was the very essence of everyday conduct. Father taught us this proverb: Ask your way and you will find the road to Rome. It was the philosophy of dependence and I often wonder whether it may not be in part responsible for the lack of real independence, and for the wide prevalence of mendicantism and pauperism in some European countries.

Again I turned to American life as a field of observation. Soon I discovered that this was not merely a characteristic of my friend who had turned in disgust from me, but a typical trait of American conduct. Then for the first time I began to see the absence of beggars from the streets; then I began to note the way poverty and pauperism are frowned upon in this country; then I learned that dependence in any walk of life is contrary to the highest form of thought and conduct in America; for *here self-reliance* and *independence are cardinal virtues.*

Above all, these years in America have taught me the power and the value of *optimism*. Here again the contrast between the old and the new is very striking. Our tendency was toward somber pessimism. Our entire environment breathed forth that point of view. Perhaps it could not have been otherwise. The death of one grandfather by poisoning and the other by drowning at sea was enough in itself to make the next and the next generation somber and sad. Mother, looked down upon by her kinsfolk because of her humble birth, led a saddened life. Father in his struggle against political corruption died almost broken-hearted, feeling that his life and ideals were not sufficiently appreciated. While in my own tossings about the world I had come to feel that this was anything but a gladsome existence.

Nor was this the whole story. The surroundings of our child-world were destined to create pessimism in our thought. We saw people burdened down by extreme poverty, their backs bent beneath an intolerable load of taxes, which reached down to the very last match they burned. Family after family was deprived of the earnings of their young men, who were snatched away into continuous wars. We saw many families all but torn asunder in this manner, while the parent emigrated to some other country in search of bread for his brood, which he could not earn at home. Added to this was the morbidness of our religious teachings. When death entered a family, the tears, the mourning, the doleful faces and somber black veils continued for years. When adversity overtook a family or any member of it, recourse was had not in seeking to recover losses or make readjustments, but in tears, tears and more tears. Our people did not know what it was to "consider the lilies of the field."

Do you believe that a person can live in such an environment during the formative years without being affected by it, perhaps for life? I am sorry to say I had been greatly influenced by this mode of thought. And the fact that during the first years of my life in America I had accidentally lived in the midst of a certain restricted and narrow Puritanical environment, only added to my original pessimistic outlook.

It was Browning who first penetrated my being with the rays of *radiant optimism;* it was he who taught me to "greet the unseen with a cheer." The optimism of American life was first strikingly illustrated to me by the hilarious and exuberant cheering of men and women over a football game. What astounded me most was to see them cheer when their team was *losing* as well as when it was *winning,* as if to say "we will yet win" and as if thereby to overcome all obstacles to victory. It was the radiant joy, the bright hope back of that kind of a cheering in life that appealed to me. When I first recognized that underlying optimism everything seemed to say: "The whole of life is a game, a game fit for joy, for expression, gladsome expression." Here again Browning says:

"Oh, the wild joys of living! the leaping from rock to rock,
    The strong rending of boughs from the fir-tree, the cool silver
        shock
    Of a plunge in a pool's living water. . . .
            .   .   .   .
How good is man's life, the mere living! how fit to employ
All the heart and the soul and the senses forever in joy."

All that these lines meant to me you can realize when you remember how again and again I had received a severe thrashing for "leaping from rock to rock" or for the "rending of boughs" and for plunging in the sea's "living water." In Italy I had been punished for the very thing that in America make up the beauty and the substance of life.

The longer I live in America the more I come to feel that *optimism is vibrant* in the very air we breathe. I find that people here have no patience with a pessimist human being. I hear people say: "Sure, this world is full of trouble . . . but, say, *ain't it fine to-day?*" I have been present at funerals where there was all the occasion in the world to weep indefinitely, but where I have seen exhibited the greatest of fortitude and optimism; I have seen people in America face all kinds of adversities with a spirit of superb courage. In peoples of the West I have seen the positive workings of this optimism in a special way. It may be that it is due in no small measure to the grandeur, the sunshine and the exuberance which God has showered in such abundance upon those vast and magnificent stretches! Whatever the reason, their optimism grips the very soul of me. I know a "Little Woman" in the West who, though she has borne endless pain and grief, still is the very embodiment of optimistic joy. I never think of her but that I think of "Pippa Passes." I remember also meeting a man once on the prairies of Colorado, who the night before had suffered a serious loss by fire,— his barns, hay and cattle,—practically all he had in life. Knowing this, as he drew near I prepared myself to listen to his sad story and to offer my sympathy. To my surprise, he had no sad story to tell, and when asked about his loss by an interested relative of his who was accompanying me, he made some brief, care-free remark and, lighting his pipe, whipped his horse and went on to the city to buy lumber to build more barns, singing and greeting the unseen as if nothing had happened. I would not say this kind of outlook on life does not exist elsewhere, but I have seen it lived in America as nowhere else on earth.

These, in a general way, are the changes which have come over my thought-life through years of residence in America. I hope I have satisfactorily answered your question. You may not think them worthy changes, but I can sincerely say that I am profoundly grateful to America and to the American people for them. I am grateful for having had the privilege of association with some real representative Americans and of rubbing shoulders with them and of absorbing something of their view of life. I am in a special way happy to have learned the English language and through its medium to have become acquainted with the stalwart thought of the master minds of the Anglo-Saxon race. Through it also I have come to know, and in a measure to appropriate, the sturdy and wholesome philosophy of the life of the American people. I am particularly grateful to those American men and women who by personal contact have brought me this awakening.

Did I say *"American men and women"?* Let us study a moment the persons to whom I have referred. The family which moved from southern California to Maine and which so impressed me with the mobility of American life was originally from England; the young lawyer was a French-Canadian; Tennyson and his "lest one good custom should corrupt the world" an Englishman; so was Browning with his freedom from the shackles of others' opinions and his optimism; my American "Big Brother" and his "brass tacks" philosophy is of Dutch descent; my friend of the "I-ask-no-favor-of-any-man" incident is a staunch Scotchman; the "Pippa Passes" referred to has a name that savors much of the fair

Emerald Isle. And so on. The only one who taught me a great lesson and who might have been said to be "natively extracted" was Lowell. Doubtless it was not their fault that I did not receive more help from people who fall in this category, but the point I want to make is this: that after all we all "came over" sometime! To me therein lies the great glory of America; that she can take the rough and unfinished material from many lands and climes and so shape it, as a master shapes his clay, that they who learn of her, who drink at the fountains of her real life, who learn to love her, *actually become different beings*.

I take my hat off to the typical American and I am profoundly grateful to have known him. Speaks he a "slanted" tongue or a mellifluent and ever so pure a brogue, so long as he is the embodiment of the spirit of America he is my man. He whose life is free to move about wherever the call is greatest; who is free from the thralldom of petty conventionalities and the nagging opinions of others; he who is idealistic and yet practical; who emphasizes worth above appearance and who greets the unseen with a buoyant cheer,—he is my man, he is my American, he is the man whom I am glad to have known, and the man whom I love with all the warmth of my Southern soul.

Your affectionate brother,
Constantine.

ПОМЕ!

Be it weakness, it deserves some praise,
We love the play-place of our early days.
The scene is touching and the heart is stone
That feels not at that sight, and feels at none.
. . . .
This fond attachment to the well-known place
Whence first we started into life's long race,
Maintains its hold with unfailing sway,
We feel it e'en in age and our latest day.

WILLIAM COWPER.

CHAPTER XIX

HOME!

FIFTEEN years had now passed since landing in this country. During all this time my people had never ceased to entreat me to return, and I had ever kept before me the dream of going back, at least for a brief visit. I had planned each year to do so, but never had enough money to make the trip. That I had worked faithfully and continuously no one could question; many times not eight or ten hours a day, but fourteen and sixteen; and I had even done night work in order to make both ends meet. I had driven myself so hard and so incessantly that vigor and health were fast slipping away. Again and again I was forced to count the pennies, wondering what further sacrifices I could possibly make that I might have just enough for a visit home. There were times when a longing for the sight of my people was almost unbearable. All that I had gone through in America would make itself felt with a tremendous accumulative power. I could again see my meager earnings being taken away from me; I could feel anew the bitter insults, the unfavorable discrimination, the ridicule, the prejudice; I could see again the prison walls within which I had been enclosed; I could experience again the pangs of hunger, the shivering cold, the hateful persecutions, the awful, terrible loneliness. My soul would almost cry out in madness for just a glimpse of those I loved and had "lost a while." With a wide ocean lying between, and with no money with which to go *and return to America,* my dream of seeing my people again was fast vanishing.

"And return to America," I said. For now I was of America. Sometimes I would wonder just how I would feel if I were suddenly placed among my relatives in Italy. Would I, after all, feel at home even for a day? Would I want to remain in Italy, should the opportunity arise, and enter some form of public life there? I did not know.

Then came the World War and thoughts something like these ran through my mind. Suppose that Italy should side with one of the powers and America with another, just where would I stand, just where would my loyalty lie? The answer came in an unforeseen manner. One day I chanced to be in Plymouth, Massachusetts. Naturally I went to visit Plymouth Rock with a group of friends. I was standing upon the Rock when patriotic emotions which I had never experienced before gripped me and a sudden revelation of all that America had stood for throughout its history and what it had

meant to me, dawned upon me in a forceful manner.
With the least possibility of harm coming to America, it was borne in upon my consciousness what She
now meant to me. America in all her fullness was
the very life of me. Later America entered the
War. One evening I was walking through the Common when I looked up and there, high above my
head, on the roof of one of the highest buildings
facing the historical grounds, and shot through with
a radiant light, I saw the Stars and Stripes,
refulgent and glorious in her streaming. Again an
inexplicable something gripped the very soul of me
and I worshiped as if at a shrine. Where would my
loyalty lie? No answer! I have often wondered
since then whether native-born Americans ever feel
anything like what I felt on those two occasions.

And it was that very vision that, by a series of
unforeseen circumstances, was to lead me back to
my native Italy. Even before America declared
war, I offered myself to the Government for military
service. When enlistments began, I twice volunteered
in the hope that, notwithstanding my defective eye, I
might get into the ranks before the authorities
should become too particular. It was one of the
most disappointing experiences of my life to be re-
jected. I still sought a possible way of serving this
country in the war. Finally, as a last resort, I
enlisted for service with the Y. M. C. A. and went
to France. I had been there about a month and a

half when I was ordered to go to Italy, with the first Y. M. C. A. party, five in all, sent to that country.

Headed by that man of magnificent spirit, Doctor John S. Nollen, formerly president of Lake Forest University, on January 3, 1918, we crossed the French-Italian border at Modane. As the train slowly wound its way down into the valley, the cold, ugly fogs of northern France gave way to the radiant sunshine of Italy. The warm sun rays were flooding the plains below. The mountains, snow-capped, stood out clear-cut as diamonds, as if God had made them that very morning. Italy was wonderful; Italy of my childhood. A flood of emotion surged through my being, warm as the sun rays, pure as the summit snows. For a time I closed my eyes; I could not bear the glory of the sight; at last I was in my native Italy! Donizetti's famous lines and strains of music came to my mind:

Oh, I-tal - ia, I-tal - ia be-lov - ed, Land of beau - ty, of sun - light and song!— Tho' a-far from thy bright skies re-mov - ed, Still our fond hearts for thee ev-er long!

It was my good fortune to visit my people soon
after my arrival in Italy. There was an important
errand to be done in connection with the American
Aviators who were then located at Foggia, and I
was detailed to do it. Naturally, since I was so
near, I seized the opportunity to visit my native
town which I had not seen for these many years.

On my way from Naples to Foggia, while passing
through that delightful country which Horace so
beautifully painted centuries ago, I sat reading a
book about that section of Italy and meditating.
Into my compartment came a man with a valise, who
from his appearance I recognized as a late comer
from America. Seeing me in the American uniform,
he at once opened a conversation in what he would
have called English. He told me he had just returned from far-off America, how many years he
had been there, what a good country it was, how
much money he had made, and so on. I do not know
whether he thought I questioned his statements, or
that I did not understand his wretched English, but
whatever the reason, he proceeded to furnish proofs
of his long residence in America. First he showed
me a dollar bill, much the worse for wear; then a
watch, an "Ingersoll," and a cheap chain. Finally,
he opened his valise and showed me several presents
which he was taking to his relatives, among others a
much-prized "Big Ben" which he was taking to his
aged mother.

We came to a small station and the man left with profuse farewells. Into the compartment came a group of five beautiful Italian young women. They were carrying books and from the conversation which I overheard, it was plain they were going to a larger village to attend high school. As they went on with their conversation, I once more took up my reading, occasionally overhearing snatches of what they were saying. Finally, I became conscious that their remarks were directed toward "that nice young American" who was reading all by himself, and of course, they thought, not understanding a word they were saying. One of the girls had a beautiful orange, hanging from a long stem with four or five leaves on it. From its freshness, it was clear that the orange had just been plucked from a tree. Their conversation continued to center round "that nice young American" and his country, America. One of them said, "Wouldn't it be nice to go to America with him?" To this all agreed. Gradually they began to joke with each other as to who would be *the one* to go. All this time, of course, I gave no indication that I understood a word they were saying. Finally, one suggested that the girl who had the orange should have the preference. And she was as beautiful a specimen of womanhood as Italy knows how to produce. They suggested that if she would only offer me her orange I would surely take her to America with me. She blushed, and to ward

off the attack which was now centering upon her,
she said: "No, I won't give him the orange, even
to go to America," but she added: "Well, I might
give him the stem and the leaves." This was more
than I could resist. So rising and walking up to
her, I made my best bow and said in as good Italian
as I could command: "Thank you, gracious
(graziosa) young lady, I will take you to America
for the stem and the leaves." The screams, the
laughter, the blushes which followed can easily
be imagined, but just then the train pulled into the
station to which the young women were going, and
they precipitately left the compartment pell-mell
amid laughter and shouts which attracted the attention of all. I stood by the window and waved
them a good-by.

The train wound its way down the mountainous
path and was soon at Foggia. I did the errand
which had brought me there, and soon was speeding
toward my native Molfetta. I had in the meantime
sent a telegram to Aunt Rose stating that I would
arrive on a certain train. The time consumed by
that journey from Foggia to Molfetta seemed like
ages. The trainman came into my compartment to
talk about America. But I led him to talk about
that section of Italy. He told me of its history,
its general contour, the location of the various cities
and villages, not knowing that I knew all about it.
Then he entered upon an account of the advance

that Italy, and especially Puglia, had made in recent years; the opening up of new railroads, the making of double track lines, the building of an aqueduct stretching for miles from the mountainous regions near Foggia through the whole length of the province, the building of electric plants, the industrial expansion of Bari, all of which was exceedingly interesting to me.

At about nine o'clock in the evening the conductor passed through the corridor and shouted "M o l - f e t t a." I took my suitcase and dismounted. No sooner had I left the train than I heard a voice in the distance shout, like an unexpected call of anguish in the night: "Costantino." No one was on the platform. The police guard was keeping every one back in the street. He scrutinized me in a special way, examined my papers, and let me pass. I pressed through a number of people who were crowding around the gate and the next moment I was in his arms. It was my good Uncle Carlo. "Zio" (uncle) I said, as he pressed me close to him and passed his hand gently over my face. "It is eighteen years almost to a day since you saw me off at this very station. I thought I should never see you again."

He took my suitcase from my hand and locking his arm within mine, led me on, as if feeling a special paternal pride. We walked in almost complete silence. It was one of those moonlight nights of

Southern Italy, when the sky is so infinitely clear and the air so balmy as to make one forget that winter ever existed. The long dark shadows of the low, flat buildings covered the narrow streets, the slender ash trees near the station and in the Villa Garibaldi, which we passed, were standing like silent sentinels as of yore. In the distance I could see the Campanile rising above the Cathedral. All was at peace. But all was changed. The shadows, the streets, the houses, the trees, the public buildings were all the same,—and yet so changed. Why did they look so small? What are these? Are they the same houses which had towered so high above my head when a boy? Are these the same streets which had seemed so spacious and which it had taken my little legs so long to traverse? Are these the same "portoni" which had seemed to my child eyes as gates to fairy castles? Are these the same trees which once had reached the very zenith of my childhood skies? Why are things so shrunken, so small? Is the Molfetta of my boyhood days after all a toy thing?

Such thoughts crowded one after another in rapid succession through my mind as I walked along by the side of Uncle Carlo. At last we reached the very house in which, with grandmother, I had spent most of my childhood and boyhood days. At the door was Aunt Rose, quivering with emotion. She, more than all the others, had been the faithful one in writing to me, in keeping in touch with all my doings in far-away America; the one who had again and again pleaded with me to return, and had offered to send me the money to do so, if I only would. Now in a moment she gave vent to all the pent-up feelings of the years. The first words she uttered, as her arms pressed me close and her warm kisses and warmer tears touched my face, were: "I thank Thee, God. I have seen him. Now I am ready to die." In the next few moments she lived over all the years since we had seen each other. Much that followed is too sacred to narrate. I was thankful that I had arrived at night, and so late that I had avoided the conspicuous attention which my uniform would have given me, and had escaped meeting the large group of friends and relatives all at once.

That night I slept in the very bed in which I had lain as a boy, with the same old posts and the same quaint canopy covering it as of old. But now it was not quite long enough for my outstretched body. I slept and I did not sleep. It seemed as if I could see my uncle going toward the balcony to fill my Santa Claus boot, as on that night long ago when I had first learned that Uncle Carlo was Santa, and I had loved him all the more. The next morning, long before I had risen, my little nephews and nieces —and it seemed their name was legion—who had learned of my arrival, tiptoed into the room in which they thought I was asleep, to view their long-

lost uncle of whom they had heard so much and
who had become the household saint of the whole
family. One after another they ran back to their
parents with descriptions of him,—how he looked,
how long he was, that his feet almost stuck out from
the foot of the bed, that he was almost bald, had no
mustaches, and had a big nose. When the reports
they had carried to their parents came back to me,
I had all I could do to recognize myself. As soon
as the long line of nephews and nieces had come to
an end, even as I was having a moment to rise and
dress, in began to file an equally long line of sisters,
uncles and aunts, and I even had to wash the shaving
lather from my face to do my duty by one of my
sisters, Agata, the jolliest of them all. In the meantime, that dear old aunt of mine, Aunt Rose, stood
by with her bosom heaving, witnessing the whole
proceeding like a sentinel, and taking a maternal
pride in what was going on.

I had scarcely had time to dress, when a "banquet"
was ready for the "distinguished" guest. I wondered how they got so many relatives into so small
a space. I was not surprised that they had sent all
the children off to play. After the dinner party,
my uncle took me out to see the town and to show
me off to it. We went to see my old nurse and the
old shoemaker who had made all my shoes in my
youth; we called upon some former pupils of my
father, now grown men and established in business.

I had now and then to accept a kiss on each cheek, which, strange to say, was not quite as pleasing to me as it should have been. I had been in America, where kisses are reserved for a special kind of creatures. We went to the mole and the harbor, both of which had seemed so enormous to me in my youth, but now were little toy things; we passed through the Villa Garibaldi, a small round patch as compared to its past splendors. The clock tower above the West gate had been torn down. Everything seemed to have shrunken to miniature size, while my boyhood friends had grown to be men, and some were gone. The "big" city of my boyhood days was no more.

My relatives and friends asked all kinds of questions about America; what the climate and the country were like; what the living conditions were there; was it true that money was in great abundance; what were the chances of good employment? They asked no questions about the government and the general life of the country. I spoke of the good things, but was too jealous of America to tell them all I knew of the life of the immigrant there, or even to hint at some of the things that I myself had gone through. They would have been shocked beyond expression to have learned that the son of Don Colì had suffered such things as I have narrated in the preceding pages. When they asked my advice about their going to America, I could not honestly counsel

them to do so. I was not unmindful of the practical
misery in which most of the poorer classes live in
Italy, but even misery is more easily endured in one's
own country. When I gave evasive answers or was
silent in the face of their persistent questionings,
they were astonished. They wondered why I would
not remain in Italy then? I shrugged my shoulders,
Italian style, and passed to the next question.

That night I again returned to the home of my
childhood and was glad that my relatives were considerate enough to leave me in the quiet of that home
with my good aunt and uncle. With them I renewed my play life. We played hide-and-go-seek
as of old; I played stealing almonds and figs as once
I used to do in earnest; I looked over all my little
books and mementoes, closely guarded by Aunt Rose
through all the years; I examined my little ships,
some of which hung on the walls; I sat in uncle's
lap and put on his nose those funny old glasses he
used to wear when he would read to me those fasci-
nating sea tales.

But through it all I was conscious, and so were
they, that a great change had taken place, deeper
and more significant by far than any mere physical
change. There were changes in training, in outlook,
in habits, in motives, which separated us forever.
Aunt Rose pleaded with me to promise that I would
remain with her, that at least I would remain in
Italy as long as she lived. She told me that the

tract of land and the "casino" on it, which she had kept for me all these years, was still mine and that I could have it for the mere staying and the mere taking. She said that she would be so happy if I would only stay with her until she died, "only a few years more." I remained silent, though not unmoved, comforting her with a word now and then. "I will come again, aunt," I said. "I will come again." She understood! I was no more of this fair clime—no more!

MY FINAL CHOICE

WORDS BY HENRY VAN DYKE.   MUSIC BY C. AUSTIN MILES.

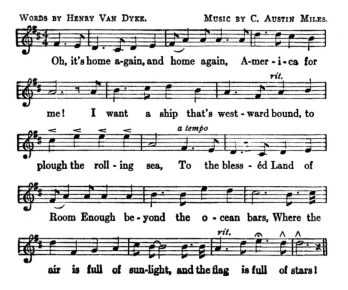

Oh, it's home a-gain, and home again, A-mer - i - ca for

me!   I   want   a   ship   that's   west - ward bound, to

plough the roll - ing   sea,   To   the bless - éd Land of

Room Enough be - yond the o - cean bars, Where the

air   is full of sun-light, and the flag is full   of stars !

CHAPTER XX

THE next morning I left Molfetta, and save for a visit of a few hours' duration which I made later, I returned to it no more. In forty-eight hours I had passed from the peaceful scenes and the reminiscences of my childhood into the throbbing activities of the most bloody war in human history. It was while in the midst of these scenes and on my own native soil, that my supreme choice was made.

I was assigned the task of projecting the work of the "Y" at the Italian front, and by a series of strange circumstances I had the privilege of close contact with some of Italy's most eminent men, both in military and civil life, and was permitted to render to Italy, in the name of my adopted country, a distinct, even though a humble, service. At Mogliano, Veneto, not far from Venice, was then located the Headquarters of the famous Third Army. Under the command of the far-famed Duca d'Aosta, this army had accomplished a prodigious feat in checking the Austrian advance in the fall of

1917, and had thereby saved Italy from further invasion and ravage. As it was only about two months since the terrible de eat of "Caporetto" had taken place, the lines of the Italian forces were just beginning to take definite shape. Under the newly appointed Commander in Ch ef, General Diaz, a general work of reconstruction was going on. As the Third Army had suffered most severely in the recent retreat, we decided to begin our work with it and to do what we could to help the authorities build up the "morale" of the men. We therefore located our first headquarters near the command of the Third Army at Mogliano.

It was my privilege, in an entirely unforeseen way, to raise the first Stars and Stripes which, to my knowledge, ever flew near the lines of the Italian army. We had been at the front about a week, when we realized the need of having our national colors flying above our headquarters. The only persons representing the United States who had up to this time made their way to the Italian front were a small group of ambulance drivers, who had taken the famous Poets' Ambulances to the relief of the Italian forces. We inquired of them about a flag, but they did not have one themselves, so could not supply us with one. We made inquiries at several places, we sent to Venice, to Padua, to Milan, but from everywhere came the answer that no Stars and Stripes were to be found. It would take three or four weeks, we were told, to have one made. Finally one day I made it known to my fellow-workers that since leaving the United States I had carried, carefully folded against my heart, a small silk flag, about eighteen by twenty-four inches in size. We decided that since we could not get any other for the present we would raise this one; and we did. We had our little ceremony and it was my privilege to put it out upon our balcony, where it remained until we had displaced it with a larger one. Later I carried that little flag, attached to my car, to the remotest spots on the firing lines and even down into Sicily, in places where it had never been seen before, I was told, and may never be seen again. Wherever it went it carried new hope and inspiration. And so it happened that it was given to an adopted American to unfurl the first American colors on the lines of his own native country during the Great War.

It was given to me to perform a still greater duty; that of carrying to the discouraged soldiers of my native country, and later to the people in the remotest spots of the interior the message of hope and encouragement from far-off America. This, too, was purely an accident. On the first Sunday we were at the front, a new Italian Casa del Soldato, or soldier's hut, was to be opened. The famous priest and patriot, Padre Semeria, was to deliver the address. On the preceding Friday it was announced that on account of illness Padre Semeria could not be present. Doctor Nollen, our chief for the whole of Italy, happened to be at the front when the news reached us, and he casually suggested to the chaplain who was in charge of the opening, that he should ask me to make a few remarks about America's participation in the war. So I was requested to speak at the opening of this first Casa del Soldato in the newly formed lines. I hesitated at first, chiefly because my practice in Italian public speaking had been somewhat limited, and I did not wish to mar the coming festivities by making a bad impression or by failing to interpret in adequate terms the ideals and the aims of America's participation in the war. However, the request was so urgent that it seemed my duty to do the best I could.

The Casa to be opened was located close to the lines. These particular regiments of "Bersaglieri," for whom the Casa was being opened, were under the command of Colonel de Ambrosi, one of the bravest and most quick-witted men of the entire Italian army. They had carried out their idealism to such a degree in beautifying an old house that they had made it into one of the most attractive spots imaginable. Around the grounds were flower beds representing the various phases of Italy's participation in the war. They had succeeded most remarkably in turning an old and dilapidated house into an architectural and landscape gem. In front of the house and camouflaged with leaves they had erected a platform which was to serve as a rostrum in the coming festivities. The time for the opening came. The air was serene and balmy, the first signs of spring were beginning to appear and the "Bersaglieri," always jovial, seemed to be in an especially good humor. The Italian soldier never forgets his mirth even under the most untoward circumstances. They had gathered in great numbers and were ready for the celebration to which they had eagerly looked forward. Our group of five American uniformed Y. M. C. A. men arrived, and it would seem extravagant were I to tell of the wild enthusiasm that burst from that group of four or five thousand men. I was escorted to the platform, where General Croce was awaiting us. When the time came, I arose to speak. Here was I, a son of Italy, for many years in far-away America, now come back to my native country to bring words of encouragement and cheer; and here I stood before them, the first man they had seen in an American uniform, and speaking the first words they had heard of America's entrance and participation in the war. I spoke for about fifteen minutes; in simple language I enumerated the reasons why America had not entered the war before, and why she had entered on the side of the Allies now; I spoke of her unbounded resources in men and means; I told them how American soldiers had already landed on European soil and that some of them would surely be sent to Italy. When I was through, wave after wave of uncontrolled enthusiasm burst from their throats. The air was vibrant with cheering. The enemy, not far distant, must surely have heard it.

When I was through speaking, General Croce met me, and in keeping with the Italian custom he kissed me on both cheeks, in token of deep friendship and appreciation. To me it seemed rather a strange performance, and looking round to my mates, standing near by, I smiled. They understood my embarrassment. The General then insisted that a picture be taken of him and myself, and another of the entire group of generals and other officers present, including our Y. M. C. A. men. These pictures were sent to the interior and published widely throughout Italy. Then a reception was tendered in the Casa to all the officers present.

So far as I was concerned, the incident was ended. To my surprise, however, the following day a messenger arrived from Army Headquarters requesting me to present myself that afternoon for a conference "regarding an important matter" with General Giuseppe Vaccari, chief of staff under the Duca d'Aosta. I went to the beautiful villa in which the command was housed and was ushered into the presence of the General. General Vaccari is a man of unusual dignity and poise, yet withal one of the most kindly men, as I came to know afterwards. As

I came into his presence, every bone and fiber of me stood erect. I did not know or even suspect what I was wanted for. After exchanging the usual greetings, he spoke of the reasons why he had called me to him. He said: "His Excellency, the Duca d'Aosta, has requested me to thank you most heartily for the service you rendered us yesterday at the opening of the Casa. We heard of the speech you made and of the enthusiasm and encouragement which it evoked in our soldiery. He further instructs me to state that he would like to have you, at the expense of the Italian Army, to continue to render such a service, by going from place to place as may be directed later, addressing the soldiers along the lines." I answered that it was my duty and privilege to render any little service I could, and that, subject to the approval of my superiors, I should be happy to place myself at the Commandant's disposal and to do what I could in the name of my country, to serve the Italian soldier. With that we parted.

From that day until I left Italy, seven months later, when I came to America to bring a message from Italy, I was in the midst of incessant activity. Repeatedly I was called, early in the morning or late in the evening, to mount a car waiting at the door and go to some spot on the lines to speak in the name of my adopted country. On one occasion it was my privilege to speak to twelve battalions of

"Ciclisti,"—the famous bicyclist sharpshooters; on another to nine battalions of the equally famous "Metraglieri di Sardinia"; one evening, just as the sun was setting, I faced a large body of men under the command of General Angelosanto, a daring Neopolitan soldier, and as soon as the address was over, they marched into the lines, not far away. On still another occasion on a hillside, on whose crest the enemy was deeply entrenched, I addressed five thousand men, who at the close of the meeting marched to their places in the trenches on the hill. And so the days passed, days of continuous activity, through which I was serving my native country in the name of my adopted country. Later at the instance of the military authorities and of the United States Committee on Public Information in Italy, I made a complete speaking tour of Sicily, reaching even the remotest hill towns inland. Sicily was at that time in a very low state of "morale," yet it rose to the occasion, and the unbounded enthusiasm of the people was manifested by the thronged theaters and other public buildings, and in the surging crowds that gathered in the open squares to hear of America. I carried with me small ribbon American flags, and distributed them by the thousands, especially to children who had relatives in the American Expeditionary Forces.

Those were the months of throbbing activity and of unequalled opportunity to observe the people

and the life of my native Italy.   I had occasion to
confer personally with scores of the highest officers
of the army, from the Duca d'Aosta to the Generals
in command of the various armies and army corps,
and with minor officers; I came into personal contact
with many civilian officers and with leaders in the
educational world of Italy.   I had the privilege of es-
corting some leading American citizens and prominent men of other nationalities to the front lines, to
interpret in some important conferences, and to
carry between certain Italian and American authorities military information of the greatest importance.
Above all, I had an unexcelled opportunity to observe the life and the institutions of my mother
country with the eyes of manhood and in a way I
never had before.   I was given access to some of
the most beautiful and cultured homes of Italy.   I
had the privilege of viewing the matchless natural
beauties of Italy and of drinking in the invigorating
sweetness of Italy's skies, rivers, lakes and seas.
Opportunities were open for me to enter public life
in my native country and to contribute to it what I
had gained of experience and outlook in my adopted
country.   At times I almost entertained the thought
of remaining in my native country.   But something
not entirely in the realm of reason or in that of
patriotic sentiment kept tugging at my heart, pulling like a magnet toward America.

One day the final choice took place.   It came in

the midst of the splendor of a military occasion and unseen by human eyes. I myself did not realize its fullest significance at the time. At Messina, where I was to address a regiment of 1918 recruits, I was met by the venerable General Lang, who took me to the summit of the hill overlooking the Straits of Messina. It was late in the afternoon, turning toward sunset, as we reached our destination. On the very summit of the hill, lined up in military array in the form of an open square, some five thousand young soldiers were awaiting our arrival. Sighting our car, officers and men came to attention, while the band wafted out on the breeze the martial strains of "L 'Inno Nazionale," the Italian National Hymn. We exchanged the usual military salutes and then in a few simple words I spoke.

While speaking, my eyes were fixed upon the matchless sight before me. In the distance beyond the strait was Scilla; there too was my native country, Italy. Below, slumbering peacefully in the sunset glow, was Messina, with her mole-arm stretching out into the sea. The crystal blue of the Mediterranean was vying with the delicate tints, now rosy, now purple, of the western sky. Subconsciously I was thinking of the Italy of the Ancients and of the Italy I had known. Before my eyes the two national standards, each exemplifying so much, were waving triumphantly in the stiff breeze sweeping over the mountain crest. One stood for Italy,

both ancient and modern, which the world respects;
for the Italy of my childhood, for all the memories
of my youth, of loved ones, for all that had been
beautiful and lovely in my boyhood; for the tender
memories of loved ones, living and dead. The other
stood for all the suffering of the years, for the
awakening of manhood, for the birth of freedom,
for the unfolding of life. I loved not one the less,
but the other more!

The address over, we exchanged greetings with
the officers in charge of the occasion and returned
to our car. Then followed a scene which will forever remain indelibly imprinted upon my memory
and consciousness. The soldiers, even before being
ordered to do so, spontaneously broke ranks and
made a mad dash toward the road, where our car
was waiting. Wave upon wave of "Evviva l'America"
swelled. They massed themselves along both sides of
the road, as our car began to move slowly down the
serpentine way. The standards were still waving triumphantly. The band was now playing "The
Star Spangled Banner." We moved on. The sun
was just going down into the sea. The waves of
cheers followed us, growing fainter and fainter like
an echo. We gradually lost sight of the soldiers,
their uniforms blending with the earth. But still
we could see a mass of white in the distance; the boys
with their handkerchiefs were waving the last pos-

sible farewell, the last "evviva" to America. All was now silent, save for the thud-thud of the engine as our car moved slowly down the hill. General Lang and I uttered not a word. Finally he broke the silence. His eyes were dim. "Memorabile!" he said as he looked back. Just then the sun sent forth its last ray. Looking back, the only thing I could see was the Stars and Stripes waving gloriously in the last radiant beam of light. I looked toward the west and in my soul I said, "Through the Western window comes the light." I knew where my heart lay.

An hour later I was on a northbound train and two weeks after that I was on my way to America. I called upon several of the civilian and military authorities to pay my respects, chief among whom was the Duca d'Aosta. He spoke deep and appreciative words of what America had done for Italy during her most trying hours, and requested me to repeat in America his appreciation whenever I had opportunity. At last I was on my way toward my adopted country. I was conscious that something vital had taken place in my life. *The final and lasting choice* had come and I knew it. Through my mind kept running the lines of Dr. Van Dyke, "It's home again, home again, America for me!" Years before, by a series of strange circumstances, I had been tossed upon the shores of America. Now I turned my steps by definite choice toward that country of which sages dreamed: AMERICA.

On September 28, 1918, sixteen years almost to a day, from the time when I first set foot on American soil, the U. S. Transport *Kroonland* anchored in New York harbor. As on the day when I had first sighted America, so now She, the Queen of the West, was again decked in festal array. It was the morning when the Victory Loan campaign was launched. The forts thundered their salutes. New York, the great city of the Western Hemisphere, was resplendent in one glorious canopy of matchless colors. I was again in America. I felt like kissing the ground, as Columbus had done centuries ago.

And yet a feeling of loneliness again came over me. Strange as it may seem, I felt as of old that I was alone. Had it not been for my American "Big Brother," whose voice over the telephone dispelled some of that feeling, I might have felt like a man without a country. Nor was this feeling without foundation, in a measure.

Soon after my return I was asked to take up work in the Middle West. A letter was shown from the man to whom I had been asked to report, saying he did not see how he could use a "foreigner" with such an "outlandish name." On my way West, a group of young men passed through the coach and taking

me for a Jew began to shout: "Sheeny, Sheeny,
how is beezness on Salem Street?" Of course within
me I laughed heartily. And yet such incidents give
one a feeling that no matter how much he is at heart
an American, he is still *different* and will forever
remain so.

I have now been in America for nineteen years; I
have grown up here as much as any man can; I have
had my education here; I have become a citizen; I
have given all I had of youthful zeal and energy
in serving my adopted country; I have come to
love America as I do my very life—perhaps more
—and yet they still call me a "foreigner." Not that
I mind it. No, no! For I believe that with a real
American a man is a man "though he comes from the
ends of the earth." I *do mind* it though for the
numberless men and women who do not know how to
take it philosophically and humorously as I do, and
who pass through life in this country under that
ugly shadow, ever hanging over their heads, of being
despised "foreigners" all their days.

As for me I care not! Though my features may
always show something of my origin, of which I
am far from being ashamed; though at times my
speech may betray my foreign birth; though I
should suffer unendingly; though Thy sons should
ever dub me a "foreigner," still I love Thee, America.
I am not blind to Thy failings, but Thy virtue and
Thy glory far outshine them. Whatever betide, I

am Thine and I claim Thee as mine own. In my veins runs blood, in my mind run thoughts, in my soul feelings and aspirations which Thou hast given me. Thy name is graven on my soul. I love Thee, Italy, my native land, with that mystic love with which men turn to their native country and as Pilgrims to their shrine. I love Thee, America, with manhood's strong love, born out of the unfolding of the mind, the evolving of the soul, the sufferings and joys, the toil and the larger loves of the years. I love Thy very life. I love Thee as I can love no other land. No other skies are so fair as Thine; no rugged mountains or fruitful plains so majestic and divine. I am of Thee; Thou art mine; upon Thy sacred soil shall I live; there I fain would die,—*an American.*

*The American
Immigration Collection*